Victoria,

From Bankrupt to $900 a Day Selling Mops

Vanessa Simpkins

Here's to Your
LOVE, EXPANSION & FREEDOM !!!

♡ Vanessa
xoxoxo

Vanessa Simpkins
St Anne Des Lacs, Quebec
JOR-1BO
Canada

www.TakeYourPowerBackNow.com
Please connect with me on facebook, twitter, linked in and youtube to keep the conversation going.

ISBN 978-09864865-0-0

Limits of Liability and Disclaimer of Warranty

Get Your Companion Audios, Video, PDF Guide & Meditation Over $597.00 Value - Yours <u>FREE</u>

Bonus #1 - FREE Audio -

"Inside Sales Tips: 5 Sizzling Strategies to Ignite More Wealth and Freedom in Your Business" - $97 Value

Featuring America's Sales Attraction Coach Vanessa Simpkins
Listen to this companion audio and discover:

1) The single most important reason why most people never excel in sales. (Never fall prey to it again!)
2) Mindset mastery. How to stop sabotaging yourself and "getting in your own way" when it comes to selling.
3) Five simple strategies that will allow you to increase your sales while having more fun than you've ever imagined possible.
4) Insider secrets to selling more authentically and effectively that will turn your sales process from "blah" to "rock your socks off" amazing.
5) Three proven methods to "close more sales more easily" for selling and marketing phobes and those who are stuck at YUK when thinking of selling.

Bonus #2 -

"Vanessa's Personal Guided Meditation & Visualization" - $37 Value

Listen to this meditation and:

1) Discover how to release emotional blocks from the energetic body quickly and easily so you can amp up your vibration with a positive frequency for success.
2) Learn exactly which organ in your body manages specific emotions and how to permanently re-program your energy system with supportive emotions.
3) Connect with the highest vision of your future self and allow your higher power to help you discover, uncover, and transform yourself into your true vision of success-guided visualization.

Bonus #3 –
"Video + PDF Guide" - $ 97 Value

Watch this video and discover:

1) Vanessa's secret weapon for manifesting with success. Learn exactly how she went from bankrupt to making $900 a day, wrote her first book, and launched a successful coaching career in less than two years all by using this simple writing exercise.

2) How to stop struggling, pushing, and forcing life to bend your way. Learn how you can apply this one simple process that takes less than fifteen minutes a day to help you attract your perfect clients, business partners, or investors, and help you close more sales more easily and make more money quickly by aligning you with what you want so it flows smoothly into your experience.

3) A step-by-step PDF guide to help you start writing your very own blueprint for success, pronto!

Bonus # 4 -
Coupon for $200 off of your
Big Breakthrough Session with Vanessa

In your Big Breakthrough Session with Vanessa you will:

1) Discover how to release your energetic blocks once and for all, and allow more wealth into your life.

2) Master the inner mindset for gaining more confidence and doubling, tripling, or even quadrupling your sales.

3) Learn how to naturally align yourself with your ideal clients so you attract your perfect clients, have more fun, and get paid for enjoying yourself and doing what you do best.

4) Develop your own unique and authentic selling style that looks and feels right for you so you enjoy the process, close more sales more easily, and make more money.

5) Conquer the outer strategies and sales techniques that will help you skyrocket your sales conversion and grow your business so you can make more money and enjoy a fabulous lifestyle with the freedom to choose how you spend your time.

Get all 6 FREE Bonuses today at
www.TakeYourPowerBackNow.com/Bonus

Bonus # 5 –
"Expert Interview with Brad Yates – Emotional Freedom Technique (EFT) Practitioner, Author, and Professional Speaker" - $97 Value

Listen to this audio and:
1) Discover how to tap into your passion and purpose using EFT (Emotional Freedom Technique), one of the most popular and effective energy psychology tool s out there!
2) Eliminate your anxiety and limiting beliefs about making money in these challenging economic times so you can start to prosper, and enjoy more money and freedom.
3) Learn a simple technique for releasing emotional resistance you can do on your own and in as little as a few minutes.

Bonus #6 –
"Expert Interview with Dr. Joe Vitale, star of *The Secret* and Spiritual Marketing Guru" - $97 Value

Get the Transcription and Accelerated PDF Work Guide to help you Achieve Success Today!
Listen to this audio and discover:
1) The real reason most people never find their passion or purpose in life, and how to overcome it quickly!
2) How a simple breakthrough clearing process will help you catapult your success in your sales career and help you grow your business like never before.
3) How to release self-sabotage once and for all in as little as seconds even if you haven't a clue that you are doing it and without spending years in therapy.

Amazon Receipt # LOVE

Get all 6 FREE Bonuses today at
www.TakeYourPowerBackNow.com/Bonus

What Others Have to Say About Vanessa Simpkins

"$30,000 In Sales 5 Weeks in A Row"

Since applying Vanessa's techniques, our sales team has hit our new goal of $30,000 … 5 weeks in a row! We know it's because of her processes our sales team had never been able to reach it's targeted goals before and certainly not 30,000! Thank you Vanessa!!

Camille Vaillancourt
www.AccesJournal.ca

"Vanessa Understands the Inner Game of Business and Life Mastery"

Vanessa helped me break through my inner blocks, realize my self worth and clarify a set of important priorities. With my new confidence, I adjusted my marketing, attracted new amazing clients and more than doubled my income! My new mindset allows me to be a better me, a better mommy, a better wife and a better businesswoman, and that's more than money can ever buy!

Sara O. Speicher, MBA
Virtual Business Manager
www.vbmpro.com

"2 Weeks and $15,000"

Vanessa pinpointed where I was holding myself back. I modeled her teachings and within two weeks, an amazing opportunity opened up. Incredibly, the same day, $15,000 was raised to support this worthy cause and carry it forward, more money following within days. ¡Un sueño hecho realidad! Thank you, Vanessa!

Mary Newswanger
www.FullPowerLove.com

"I Quadrupled My Income Because of You!"

Vanessa has changed my life in ways I can't even begin to describe! Before I met her I was totally dissatisfied with my life, in debt, and hopping from job to job.

Following her lead and this contagious happiness she exudes has literally turned my life right around to the point where I don't even recognize myself.

I've quadrupled my income, lived my dream, and traveled to Hawaii. Most of all I know (really know!) how to manifest whatever I want. Vanessa, I just want to say thanks from the bottom of my heart!

Melanie Layer
Regional Sales Trainer
St. Jerome, Quebec

"My Pockets Are Full of Cash!"

Vanessa was the one I'd call for help when I felt like giving up, throwing in the towel, and saying *adios*! I want to say thank you for always making me feel better and helping me turn my mood around quickly so that I'd walk away from my day with pockets full of cash!

Sophie Protopoulos
Sales Representative
Montreal, Quebec

"Vanessa, You Are a Rare Breed Indeed!"

Vanessa is absolutely extraordinary! Her sales-per-day tripled that of previous vendors in our store. I have never witnessed anything like it before, and I must say it is much to our welcome relief – especially in this challenging economy.

Vanessa's shows are captivating, her energy is dynamic, and people fall in love with her genuine manner of making her shows so much fun and interactive. She has a wonderful way of making people fall in love with her and just want to eat her up with a spoon! Vanessa, you are a rare breed: a mixture of fun, positive charisma, and success.

Marianne Cocks
Associate Store Director
Quebec

"My Business Has Been Profoundly Affected!"

Vanessa is a force of nature. The closest way I can describe her is: the spirit of charisma, intention, and growth.

While Vanessa has an amazing charisma, she's also very intelligent, and she has had great experience and results in developing and manifesting desires and sales. Vanessa has brilliant ideas on how to grow things – dreams, relationships, businesses – and she showed me how to put them immediately to good use.

My life and my business have been profoundly affected by her and the processes she has led me through.

Darren Stamos
Inventor
Toronto, Ontario

"A Champion of Direct Marketing!"

We have had the chance to work with Vanessa on several occasions here at our store promoting her products.

She is simply incredible, and her sales are phenomenal! Among all of the sales presenters we have worked with, hands down, Vanessa is the best. She is in a class all her own.

She makes her sales presentations truly dynamic and interactive. She delivers with such enthusiasm that the clientele are always in rapt attention of her every word.

I have to tell you that she has impacted our store in more ways than you can imagine, as our professional salespeople working here in the store on a regular, day-to-day basis have integrated several elements of Vanessa's sales and marketing techniques with surprising success.

Alain Fortin
D.A.M.
Sears Sherbrooke, Quebec

Dedication

To my biggest inspiration in life who taught me to do what you love and love what you do! I dedicate my first book to my father, Ron Simpkins (1942–2008), professional artist, best friend, and creative genius of massive proportions! Thank you for having the courage to be who you are, and thank you for always believing in me.

Acknowledgments

I am so blessed to have so many wonderful people who love and support me! To all of the fabulous people in my life who love, support, and believe in me: thank you!

Best gypsy, fly-by-the-seat-of-your-pants soul sister anyone could ever have, Cristina.

Mom, you live wire, I love you.

Wonderful, loving, sometimes-nutball family: You know who you are!

Marci Lebowitz, word designer extraordinaire. My guiding light and intuitive genius.

Best friends and special peeps I hold so close to my heart: Georgia laudi, Claudia Chalabi, Mona Gaucher, Janis Johnston, Joanie Simpkins, Sabine Macdonald, Darren Stamos, Marianne Cocks, Lucy MacDonald, Anita Rudichuk and Nathalie Morin.

Lori Couture, for recognizing a great mop lady when she sees one.

Julie Conner, one of the most fun, free, and authentic women I know with a legendary Hawaiian bathhouse!

Donna Kozik, creator of "Write a Book in a Weekend" event for helping me get this book off the ground.

Miranda Lightstone, editor with finesse, thank you for all of the hard work and hours you've put into this project. I could not have done this without you!

This book is dedicated to all of the courageous people who take life by the horns and move confidently in the direction of their dreams. Full Power to Your Success!

About the Author

"Authenticity is the new currency in business today."

- Vanessa

Vanessa Simpkins is a sky rocket your confidence & cash flow mentor, speaker and author of "From Bankrupt to $900 a Day Selling Mops". Creator of the "Transformational Breakthrough Summit" Vanessa helps entrepreneurs breakthrough their inner blocks, skyrocket their confidence and put proven systems in place to attract more clients and make more money. She's been featured in "Motivated Magazine", "Today's Business Women Magazine", worked alongside personal development experts like Joe Vitale from the hit Movie "The Secret" & Marci Shimoff from "Happy for No Reason" and has also spoken at the TED EX "Let's Spread Success" event in Montreal. Vanessa loves teaching authentic success principals that empower and inspire **Personal & Professional FREEDOM ** to help entrepreneurs & sales professionals create a life and business by design instead of by default. To find out more about her workshops in Costa Rica, USA and Canada and to get your FREE audio "How to Sky Rocket Your Confidence & Cash Flow: 5 of the Biggest Money, Mindset and Power Leaks Entrepreneurs Make and How to Avoid Them" visit her websitewww.TakeYourPowerBackNow.com.

Contents

Introduction

People ask me what I do for a living, and I tell them I fly around on a broomstick and sell mops! Everyone laughs, of course, until they find out I'm serious. Then they don't know whether to laugh or cry. They ask, "No, seriously. What do you do?" Really, I tell them. I sell mops!

I didn't always sell mops. In my teens I sold beer as a bartender, got frustrated, and wanted a real job, so I jumped on a plane and taught English in Osaka, Japan, when I was 20 years old. I later wound up with my knapsack living on the beaches of Thailand doing yoga for breakfast every morning with a guy who looked like Osama Bin Laden. I enjoyed it so much that I stayed there for four months.

The truth is, society sells you into this perverse vision of happiness, telling you that if you work really hard and make enough money then you'll be happy. I bought it – hook, line and sinker – and I was no happier. There I was, 21 years old, living in a beach hut bungalow overlooking the ocean with no electricity and no running water, living with this huge, hairy spider. And guess what? That was the happiest I have ever been. I had given it all up. I sold my car, put my gorgeous Victorian apartment up for rent, and quit my job as a bartender making great money. Who needs money, anyway? I was miserable inside. I left my loving boyfriend – everything.

I'm sharing all of this with you because it is the reason I got into sales in the first place. It wasn't to become an expert salesperson or sales guru. The reason I got into sales was for the freedom it allowed me to experience life.

The truth is, I've been in a panicked sort of rush to find my life's work for as long as I can remember. And the big, fat cosmic joke is that the harder I tried to figure it out – to force it to work – the more confused, frustrated, and overwhelmed I became.

I came home from my big trip to Asia and brought with me a new awareness. I wanted to live my life with as much happiness and freedom as possible. The Western world, I had decided, was completely screwed up and had its priorities all backward, chasing money in pursuit of fulfillment.

Yoga transformed, uprooted, and replaced my chronic nervous chaotic condition with a peaceful and confident knowing that all is divinely guided and divinely timed to support us in life, in our favor, always. I had more clarity.

What I wanted more than ever was to make a lot of money and have way more fun and freedom doing it. So I got into sales and started selling my dad's high-end paintings. That was fine for a while, but I was too dependant on Dad to paint them. I got into selling advertising and found out that the guy I worked for was a crook and was robbing people out of their money, using it to build his dream home and not delivering on the product he promised. So that didn't last long either. I high-tailed it out of that job and decided if I was going to have any chance at success I'd better go into business for myself. That's exactly what I did.

I became a weight-loss coach. Against all the warning from friends and family, I joined a multi-level marketing company and in under two years declared bankruptcy. So much for faking it till you make it.

I was up shit's creek without a paddle. Looking back, I just wasn't prepared for all that was involved with running and managing a business as an entrepreneur. Learning sales and marketing was a whole new ball game, and by the time I finally figured it out I was in so much debt I was afraid to pick up the phone when it rang because of daily threats from the collection agencies.

I moved into my boyfriend's tiny one bedroom and one bathroom apartment he called "the Bronx." It was in a lousy neighbourhood and was a musty basement apartment. We crammed everything we could from my huge six bedroom and one bathroom into "the Bronx." We stacked boxes high to the ceiling with just a trail to get in the door and to the bed. I remember the fridge door wouldn't open all the way because there were just too many boxes piled everywhere.

The big turning point came for me one night when our neighbors, a couple in their 50s, kept me awake all night. They were dirt poor, and picked fruit and other menial jobs for money that they drank away in the evening outside on the front steps of the Bronx. The man was almost blind, and after a few beers would start ranting and raving and falling all over the place, knocking things over and making all kinds of noise.

I remember lying awake that night in the Bronx thinking to myself, "Jesus, how in the hell did I wind up here?" You know that moment when you've just had enough and make a decision that, no matter what, life will be better and you'll find a way no matter what? I was determined, and I was also so afraid that if I didn't do anything I would end up like that poor couple one day: drinking away my miseries. Not an option, I told myself.

At that point I was working as an acupressure practitioner and massage therapist at a holistic center. I took a course called "Create Your Life" and sunk my teeth heavily into Law of Attraction.

In less than a year I attracted my mop job and was on a plane to Hawaii, living my dream on the beach again. I had finally mastered sales and marketing. I was making a ton of money. I was selling lint removers at the time. I hadn't graduated to mops yet, but life was great. I was on vacation with my sister, island-hopping in Hawaii. Then all of a sudden, Dad died.

Shit balls.

My father's passing was a huge inspiration to "get the show on the road, kiddo," as he would say. I needed to stop playing small, get out there, and get my message out to the world – get cracking, because life is short and before you know it you're dead.

I had the very rare opportunity to live free and experience what true freedom and true success were with Dad. He was an artist who painted nature. He was an authentic, genuine, creative, and easygoing guy who took us along on his long summer painting trips to the coast, where an afternoon of work would leave my sister and I catching frogs by a pond, or lazing on the beach while he captured his favorite water lilies on canvas.

Dad died of a massive heart attack outside in nature – a true testament of his life's work – with a smile on his face. Nice exit there, guy. What a way to go, right? When I die, I hope I have a smile on my face.

I had even more pressure to find freedom, happiness, and wealth in my life. I kicked my mop job into high gear, went on a craze of personal development seminars, and started making a lot of money. Yes, incredibly, sometimes $900 a day. I became the top salesman for a major company in 2009, and they paid for two all-inclusive trips for me: one to Mexico and one to the Bahamas. I had more freedom than anyone else in the company. I regularly took off two and three months to travel the world, doing what I love: hiking mountains, immersing myself in nature, hunting for seashells and crystals – bliss.

None of it would have been possible without mastering sales and marketing. A lot of entrepreneurs and sales professionals could benefit from my sales experience and started asking me for help. Everyone told me to write a book about my hilarious mop job antics. Voila – here it is!

In this book you'll learn how to look at sales as a spiritual practice and how to be more authentic and effective in your business. That's the secret to my success: authenticity. Now more than ever, people want to do business with people they can connect with – people who are real and transparent. This book will teach you how to tap into your authentic self so you can attract all of the necessary people, circumstances, and events to help you create more wealth and freedom in your life. You'll learn exactly how to apply the law of attraction to blast your sales through the roof. And you'll also learn some of the outer mechanics– the more tangible and practical knowledge of how to create an amazing offer that delivers real value to your customers so they love you forever and want to do business with you again and again.

Chapter 1

How You Sabotage Your Success in Sales: Is This Book for You?

If you are a sales professional, entrepreneur, coach, or consultant you know that sales is the core of your business. It doesn't matter how amazing your product or service is; what matters most is how many other people think it's amazing, too.

By mastering the sales process you not only enjoy more money and freedom in your life, but also reach a bigger audience with your message. You develop an unbreakable confidence that is highly attractive – even addictive to people.

This book is for you especially if you have to give sales presentations in front of people, whether a board room of executives or a handful of prospects at a hotel meeting. Even if you sell to people individually through consultations over the phone or in person, whether you sell products or services, you will benefit from the information provided in this book.

My intention is to help you gain more inner confidence and presence, as well as the outer skills you will need to help you close more sales more easily so that you can enjoy more freedom in your life and in your business.

When you can master the sales process, you will have more money. Having more money in your business means you have more options so you can expand and grow more easily, too.

If you've tried to sell your products and services in the past and have come up short on the profitable results you had hoped for, you understand there are some challenges involved both on an inner and outer level.

Challenges You've Faced in Sales

1. **Selling is hard work. It's manipulative, pushy, and aggressive. I just don't have what it takes to be good at it.**

    Have you ever been afraid to tell people that you are in sales? People just seem to wrinkle their noses when you mention *sales*. "Oh," they say as a blank stare comes across their faces and they change the subject quickly, afraid that you'll try and sell them something.

    You've probably heard that 95% of small business owners go out of business within the first five years. This, I believe, is primarily because entrepreneurs don't prioritize their time efficiently and don't engage in activities that harvest the most important asset to the company: money!

    Most people hate the idea of selling. They love being creative but hate prospecting for clients, marketing, and selling. Most entrepreneurs I interviewed are resisting and struggling through their sales process or winging it through by chance.

    Without the proper system in place to turn your prospects into paying clients, selling becomes as effective as trying to shoot a bull's eye while being blindfolded.

    What if there was a way to sell without selling? What if your clients sold themselves on your products and services, and all you did was hold their hands through the process?

    The truth is, people love to buy but hate to be sold to. Let me show you how you can sell without selling by strategically targeting and attracting the right clients and then leading them through a process that gets them to raise their hands and scream, "I want it!" And have them take action to buy right away!

2. **No one is buying. The economy is in the dumps. There's no money out there. People are broke, and no one is spending money.**

There's doom and gloom all over the nightly news and everywhere you look. The recession is like the flu virus, hiding in the darkness; you wake up at night in a cold sweat dreaming that you lost your shirt. Was it just a dream?

Maybe you lost that cozy nest egg when the recession hit and you're now faced with a completely different set of career options or job options. And sales – well, there's always a job in sales somewhere.

The truth is, I've made the most money in my career *yet* with the economy in a recession. I wasn't selling something people needed, either; I was selling a mop. You know, you can buy a mop at a dollar store.

I was selling the Rolex of mops – the Bentley of mops: $40 plus some refill mop pads. You were lucky if you got to the cash register with less than $100 of microfiber mop paraphernalia under your arm.

I worked in mining towns where half of the city had no work from the mines closing down in northern Ontario. So what? I still mopped up on cash!

How did I do it?

I had the proper mindset.

There will always be someone crying over spilled milk. Don't cry; invent a way to clean up the milk. You can always make money. Prosperity comes from having the right mindset.

In this book I'm going to share with you my system for attracting all of the right clients, opportunities, and experiences you desire to ignite your success starting today!

3. I can't find clients to sell to.

So, you want to advertise yourself. You need to find clients to fill your sales funnel. Where do you look to spend your advertising dollars?

You need to learn how to market your products and services - one to many in order to be efficient and leverage your time. You want to find partners both on-line and off-line who will help you generate leads for your business.

You want to make sure that you use your time effectively, because time is money. If you are wasting your marketing efforts on the wrong people or in the wrong way it could lead to detrimental losses. I know; I went bankrupt figuring out a profitable way to sell.

I'm sure you'll agree that if you can leverage the same efforts you do now for more profit, your career will become extremely exciting.

4. I just don't have the confidence to be good in sales.

The first things I hear from people when I tell them how much money I make selling mops are: "Oh, I could never do what you do," and "Wow. Sales is such a tough job. I'm terrible at sales." The resistance is almost immediate. People are preconditioned to believe that you have to be a weasel to persuade people to buy . The truth is, you can be great at sales even if you hate the idea of selling.

If you like people and have a passion for something, you can share that in an authentic way. When you learn how to do this by simply practicing, you gain killer confidence – and that confidence isn't just in your ability to sell, but more your ability to communicate well with others.

Confidence is something that comes from doing. Most people have the idea that when they *feel* confident then they will do it.

I know what it feels like. I still get the sweats before I go on stage in a new store. My heart starts racing, and I think: "What if they don't laugh at my jokes? What if they hate me?" It's silly, really.

Fear is always a part of it, and you learn to ignore it and push through it.

If you let fear stop you, you never get anywhere in life.

When I really just let loose on my mop stage, and forgot all about my fears and just did it, I learned that even if you screw up, you learn something – and you don't die. Imagine that.

Confidence comes through practice. Sales is like learning how to ride a bike or learning how to cook a yummy meal. You might fall down and scrape a knee, or ruin an entree with too much salt. So what? If you try it again, one day soon you'll be squealing with delight, having fun with a full tummy and a full bank account to boot.

I'll give you some tips to help you keep moving forward no matter where you feel you are stuck. These are some of the energy psychology tools I use on a daily basis, and I am sure you will find them super helpful as well.

The Least Glamorous Job

"Do not go where the path may lead; go instead where there is no path and leave a trail."
                                                          – *Ralph Waldo Emerson*

Okay, I admit that selling mops is probably the least glamorous job out there. It's certainly not my passion and purpose in life! However, I will say that doing live presentations in big, retail chain stores and selling mops taught me more about sales and public speaking than any seminar, book, or program ever could. In under two years I crawled out of personal bankruptcy and went from earning $300 a week to $900 a day. I mastered the sales process, and no one can ever take that away from me. Once you know sales, you know sales. It's like riding a bike. Once you learn you never forget!

I won't lie to you: Selling mops is the most challenging job I have ever had. Here is what a typical day looks like for me selling mops: You're shopping in Sears when all of a sudden you hear a booming voice over a loud speaker announcing free gifts in the store. What do you think? "Oh, what's this about? Someone is trying to sell me something." Right? You might go over to this "special" location filled with curiosity, but inside you vow to grab the gift and run, right? Come on, be honest here. That's what I would do!

So, my job selling mops is to attract, confront, charm, and then sell a mob of highly skeptical people, day in and day out, over and over and over again. Not an easy task! On a typical day, I do six to eight mini demonstrations that would last anywhere from fifteen to twenty-five minutes and average me an income of $500–$900 a day.

I'm not telling you how much money I make to impress or brag. To some people, $900 a day is a fart in a windstorm. But to me it's some good money. I say all of this because the drop-out rate for this job is very high, simply because most people aren't willing to learn from rejection.

Most people take failure personally, and this prevents them from mastery. I say, look at selling like an experiment. See what works and what doesn't.

I can't tell you how many times I've completely blown a show. I would be standing there in the middle of the store at the end of my presentation with a crowd of people standing around me, staring at me blankly. No sound at all – well, maybe crickets chirping. Can you say uncomfortable? Isn't that your worst fear? I can't tell you how many times I have let fear rob me of success.

Maybe you're a bit like me: afraid of failure. Or you're afraid of screwing up and feeling like a fool when you don't make the sale. No one likes rejection. It's normal to feel off at first, but don't let fear prevent you from earning the money you deserve.

The best advice I can give you is to look at your selling process and the money you now earn as your results, and decide to become a mad scientist. Find out what is working and what isn't, and continually ask yourself: "How can I make this easier?" Test it out, tweak it here and there, and try it again a different way.

You know what they say: If you really want to grow, open your own business. It's personal growth from the inside out! Your business can only grow to the extent that you do personally because your business is just an outer extension of you.

"You are fortunate if you have learned the difference between temporary defeat and failure; more fortunate still, if you have learned the truth that the very seed of success is dormant in every defeat that you experience."
– Napoleon Hill

Chapter 2

Sales as a Spiritual Practice

I know these two words – sales and spiritual – are probably two words you'd never think to put together in the same sentence, but I have to say that the old model in sales and business is dying.

By dying, I mean that the whole notion that selling and salesmen, and really anything to do with sales, is inherently linked to some slimy used-car-salesman approach that entertains words like struggling, fighting, pushing, controlling, fear, manipulation, and anger. The traditional salesman technique of forcing or convincing people to do something against their will through trickery and manipulation is over.

This idea that "you have to close-close-close the sale" and "optimize effectiveness at all costs" is being replaced with a new emphasis on building relationships, developing brand loyalty, and being authentic and transparent in your business.

Everything is changing in this new world, as the old world of the illusion of separation falls away and sheds light onto the inclusion-based Universe where everything is intimately connected and seamlessly woven together.

What I mean by "illusion of separation" is the illusion that we are separate from our environment. The illusion is that we are separate from each other – that my thoughts won't hurt or harm others. It is an illusion we suffer from because everything is energy and everything is connected. What you put out there in terms of energy, thoughts, or emotions has a ripple effect on the quality of your life and your level of prosperity.

By now, everyone has heard of, read the book, or watched the hit film The Secret, which speaks about the Law of Attraction and several universal laws that govern our reality.

People are awakening to their inherent power to create, instead of being victims of circumstance, and this notion is shifting the way we do business as well as our models for selling.

Attracting the right clients, partners, and favorable opportunities is part of this movement. The emphasis is on change from within – a connection to a higher set of values, community, honesty, and authenticity at all costs.

What I realized while selling mops was very profound: I realized that life is like a mirror. No matter what I believed about my crowd, about the store I was working in, about the people I was serving, or about the product I was selling, whatever I believed I re-created.

The only thing that really is true is what you believe. A belief or assumption about reality or your perception of it, affects your actions and therefore the results that you will see.

My mop stage became a testing ground for my subconscious beliefs. Test, test, test; that's all I did. I looked at what transpired through my shows, who showed up, and what results I achieved. I asked myself, "Okay, what was going through my mind there? How did I create that? How did I do? Did I pass today's tests? Was I living from joy and happiness? Did I face my challenges with confidence and honesty, or did I blame some outside circumstances for my results? Did I celebrate my achievements, or did I beat myself up for not being where I think I should have been? How much fun did I have? How much money did I make?"

Looking at sales as a spiritual practice requires you to take full, 100% responsibility for everything that shows up in your business and everything that doesn't!

At a T. Harv Eker Millionaire Mind Seminar I attended years ago (which I highly recommend you go to as well if you haven't already; it's free; it will blow your mind), Harv said two things that really stuck with me:

1) If you want to make money, get a job that pays you on commission, because then you will be able to measure your progress and success by how much money you make.

2) Everything is energy. Sales is just an exchange of energy. Learn how to manage your energy, and, when people show up, charge them!

Now, I know you're thinking to yourself, "There's nothing spiritual about that last bit!" However, in reality, that is what sales is: an exchange of energy between two people.

The journey toward spirituality is the journey toward authenticity. In sales, authenticity is what sells.

People want to do business with people who are transparent, true, open, and honest. They want people who feel good to them. You can't feel good to other people when you don't feel good to yourself, right?

When you are in that present moment – not worrying about the past failures you've had, not frustrated about how things haven't panned out for you before – you are fully engaged and present. You have power. You are in what I call your Full Power Presence or what some artists call the creative flow.

It's simply electrifying, and if you can tap into that while you're selling – if you can get out of your head and away from all of the fears surrounding your ability to sell and get into that space – then you will mop up on cash like nobody's business!

No one else is teaching you about sales this way. Looking at sales as a spiritual practice is a revolutionary way to view your role in sales and in business.

Mastering the journey to authenticity and tapping into your Full Power Presence is the way to lasting wealth. The journey will not only bring you a lot of money, but a lot more joy, peace, and happiness as well. And that is something to celebrate!

Old-World Sales vs. New-World Sales

Our culture has not taught us to love and share openly or to give willingly in order to receive either in our personal lives or in business. It has taught us to protect ourselves – to look out for ourselves first and foremost.

What transpires is an energy of competition.

The work of sales is shifting from the old-world view of competition to the new-world view of unity.

Success will be measured not by how much you can do, but by how happy you are doing it. When you are connected to your higher self, standing in your authenticity – what I call your Full Power Presence – and acting from that space of self acceptance, love, and confidence, then the whole world comes rushing in to help you.

Whether that rush be in attracting new business, closing a sale, or building a team of leaders, remember that connection with self = connection with success.

Here is how the old world in business and sales is shifting over to the new-world view of interconnectedness and selling from a space of love and authenticity.

Old World	New World
Following strict guidelines, scripts, and stiff protocalls.	Injecting your authentic voice and your intuitive presence into the mix.
Creating better tactics, promotions, and marketing materials.	Creating the inner foundation of strength, presence, confidence, and self-love because that is what people really buy from you.
Manipulating and hypnotizing, forcing, and pushing people to buy.	Being real, authentic, and fun. Sharing, teaching, and giving so that people step up and say, "Yes, I want that!" Delivering on value is at the core of the sales process.
Sell it to them no matter what. Close, close, close is the aim of the sales interaction.	The aim is to have fun and feel good, no matter what. Because it's all in the relationship, cultivating harmony and good feelings. That is what sells.

Used car salesman: sleazy and cheesy. "Buy this because I say so" models.	Helping buyers decide that your product or service is a really good fit for them. Recognizing that everything comes back to you, and cultivating harmony and not profit at the expense of others.
Mass-market promotions geared at everyone to get as many people as possible the biggest bang for my marketing buck.	Targeted promotions to niche markets and fewer people who you understand and can actually serve. Smart marketing and language that speaks to and engages the buyer's core. A need to address objections right away so that you make it easy for them to buy and feel good.
"How can I get them to buy?" attitude.	"How I can serve?" attitude
"How can I lure them in and trap them?"	"How can I attract them?"

Sales is an exchange of goods and services for money.	Sales is an exchange of energy where money is the quantifying result of how much value you delivered, how unique your offer was, and how well you were able to connect and engage your audience with love.
Rush, rush, rush to close as many sales as possible with a fear-based mentality.	There is enough time for everything: enough clients, enough energy, and enough of every-thing in the universe. It is abundant. So I will be present, relax, and enjoy the ride.
Fear-based competion and lack mentality to drive sales. Greed for money is running the show.	Sharing an important and compelling message is at the core.
Pushy, manipulative model of sell-ing. Trying to convince people to buy.	Attracting buyers by offering valuable content, services, products, and great offers that dis-tinguish you and differentiate you from what everyone else is doing in your market. Creating a buzz and attracting a swarm of happy clients.
Hook-and-sell basis where you talk about benefits, benefits, benefits and don't really deliver content or teach; you just hook and sell them.	Value-based and free trial lead to the customer making his own decision to buy on the basis that what has been sampled and taste-tested is fabulous, and now he wants more.

Whereas before, entrepreneurs were mostly driven to perform and act by the money their actions promised, now they are driven to discover by happiness, by what feels right, and by what is aligned with their core values. Yes, money is important, but it's not the only goal.

The purpose is a lifestyle that allows for freedom to enjoy what's important, such as family, friendships, and experiences of connection and unity. People are becoming more and more aware of how they feel and are placing an emphasis on creating extraordinary lives and cultivating true happiness.

So the questions become: "How do I prepare for and protect and build a business model for myself that will sustain these changing times and flourish right alongside these monumental leaps of evolution? How do I make money while maintaining good will to others, and deliver solid value? How do I apply spiritual principals in my business, in my job, and throughout my sales process to achieve greater good for all and for my ultimate prosperity and happiness?"

Managing Your Energy

The problem with looking at sales as a spiritual practice is that you have to look at all the ways you contribute to the problems you are facing. That can be very frustrating. The good news is you have control over yourself, and the energy you put out – your energetic field, your aura, or whatever else you want to call it. You have to be 100% responsible for what you put out there because that is what you attract back in to yourself. If you are angry, you will most likely attract angry clients. If you have a poverty mindset, then you attract broke clients, and so on.

I'll share a story that demonstrates quite well how this all works. I was so happy flying home from a six-week vacation in New Zealand. I had visited my wild and crazy adventure tour-guide sister, and we had gone bungee jumping and visited wineries. We went trekking in nature all over the place, and I thought I was so smart because I had escaped winter! Or so I thought.

I realized the next day while driving to work, freezing in my car, that I had come home way too early. Well, I was ranting and raving in my car to myself about how bloody cold it was back in Canada. I worked myself into an angry frenzy about this, and if you are apt to working yourself up into a frenzy you know how simple it is. Before you know it, you're acting out some ludicrous scenario that has never happened before, and probably never will, just for the sake of it.

I got to work and did my first announcement, and this big, brawny woman in her 50s showed up bellowing in a loud, angry voice: "What is this? I have to watch some stupid show! Jesus, I can't believe I came all the way up here for this?!" She was livid, just as mad as I had worked myself up in the car. And then it hit me: Oh, no! I created this!

If you're into the Law of Attraction, then you know how this works. Like energy attracts like energy. I had let myself get angry that morning and allowed it to spew out of me like venom all the way to work. And the first show I did, there was this angry woman to deal with. I had to deal with her because you know how people are: like sheep, right? One person gets an idea, and before you know it the entire group thinks the same thing.

It's not enough to manage my own energy; I have to manage the group energy as well. If I fail at that, I don't make money, because selling mops is a job that pays only on commission.

Luckily, by my ignoring that woman, she eventually got bored with trying to ruin my show because I wasn't reacting to her nuisance and left. Phew!

Call to action: How you manage your energy daily affects your sales. Do you allow yourself to engage in mindless chatter or give yourself in to anger often? Do you feel like you have no control over your emotions? If someone says no to you, rejects you, or downright attempts to tear you down, do you let it get the best of you? Does your mood or your day often get ruined by little things? Do little things turn into big things for you?

These are very good questions to ask yourself. Honesty will bring you awareness, and that it is the first step toward attracting more ease and prosperity in your business. This is about being responsible and managing your energy. We'll get into specific details about how you can do this in Chapter 3.

If you're out of control, I'm going to teach you how to get back into your power by managing your energy properly. For now, just keep in mind that whatever your energy is doing inside you gets sprung back at you from the outside world, just like a mirror.

Love vs. Manipulation and Fear

In his book Spontaneous Evolution, Bruce Lipton, cellular biologist, sheds new light on the nature of reality, proving that science has had it all wrong.

Evolution occurs not from the Darwinian model of survival of the fittest – the exaggeration of competition – but actually from coming together in unison and partnership. That is how leaps of evolution occur. What we teach kids in science class today is false and creates an "us against the world" mentality instead of an "us with the world" mentality.

Einstein said: "The field is the sole governing force." The energetic field that is all around us activates, creates, and shapes our physical reality. As humans, we have the capacity and power to direct energy through our thoughts. Our thoughts affect the way we feel through emotions. And emotions are vibrating fields of energy.

Guess what? The heart is the most powerful organ that creates frequencies and magnetic fields through emotions. It isn't just mere coincidence that ancient traditions teach that the heart is the center of the universe. Jesus said that if you can feel it in your heart, it will be.

In yoga you learn about the heart chakra as being the chakra that connects the energy of the heavens with the energy of the earth.

In Chinese medicine they teach that the "spirit lives in the blood of the heart."

Science is now proving what ancient wisdom has been teaching for thousands of years. It is an exciting time indeed, and a confusing time for those people who don't have the courage to get on the love boat.

We've just been so disconnected from it while we chase money and climb the social ladder that we've neglected ourselves in the chase for success.

Most people want what they can't have. They are locked into struggle, shame, guilt, fear, anger, and a dozen other limiting beliefs that keep them from experiencing prosperity through authentic presence and love.

This doesn't follow the linear model for achieving success. This is a heart-centered conscious approach to business that is very different. It's radical and unique. It's based on the heart sending the impulse through emotions and then the mind executing its endeavours instead of reacting to the constant mind chatter, fear of lack and limitation that drive most people's actions.

One day, in Buckingham, Quebec, while I was doing my mop shows, I came upon this idea that sales is really just engaging people into the realm of possibility, and that a truly great salesman doesn't convince, but is present enough in this power of self-love to make an irresistible offer stand in the knowledge that this product/service is fabulous. He can then hold the space for people to decide for themselves that they want it. There is no manipulation involved.

Here's a great offer. Here's how it will help you. Try it out. Buy today and you get this cool bonus. You're going to love it. You can try it risk-free and return it if you don't like it.

All is said and done in a delightful manner where the emphasis was on having fun, not selling.

"There is only one way under high heaven to get anybody to do anything. Did you ever think about that? Yes, just one way. And that is by making the other person want to do it. Remember there is no other way."
– Dale Carnegie

In today's world you are rewarded for really caring about your customers. Really caring means really understanding them – being presently focused and available to give to them; being balanced and authentically communicating with them comes from this presence that love delivers. If you really love yourself, you can love your clients, and then you will love your lifestyle because you'll really mop up on cash!

I noticed that when I was on my mop stage – sometimes just laughing with the crowd, listening to people make jokes, then making jokes myself, and engaging with them – answering concerns and being present would help me sell like crazy!

Other times when I was tired, hungry, worn out, not in the mood, and feeling like I had to do another show, then people could feel my lack of desire. They could just sense that I was ripping away my script, or running on empty and wasn't engaged. You can't engage others unless you come from this space of self-love first.

Call to action: Pay attention to your emotions and what your body is telling you. Pay very very close attention to your needs. Your body talks to you all of the time. We've been taught to ignore our needs and push our physical limits to exhaustion in exchange for being productive, effective, and profitable.

You can't be any of those things if you don't feel good, or if you have health concerns that are being ignored. When you look at highly successful and present people, they are usually well balanced and very healthy because they have understood the importance of "feeling good."

Listen to your body talk. Are you pushing yourself too hard? Do you get enough sleep? Are you hungry? Do you need a break? What is your body telling you about your present needs? You can't help other people with their needs until you fulfill yours first. That is self-love.

Chapter 3

The First Three Insider Strategies

How to Use the Law of Attraction to Boost Your Bottom Line from "America's Sales Attraction" Coach

No. 1: ASK

Take the responsibility to see clearly what you want through contrast and create intentions.

No. 2: BELIEVE

Reinforce by visualization, writing, and emotionally anchoring experiences in the body.

No. 3: RECEIVE

Allow it to materialize through feeling good and consistent gratitude.

This is a powerful three-step process that you can start using immediately to start attracting more prosperous opportunities, experiences, and fabulous clients who love and appreciate you. It could even result in a thrilling new career, a wonderful job you enjoy, or anything else your heart desires.

This is a recipe you can use in any area of your life, but for the purpose of this book I'm going to focus on how you can use the Law of Attraction to boost your bottom line in business so you mop up cash.

If you can master these three steps to use the Law of Attraction to benefit you, then the state of the economy will never be a worry for you again. Remember: There are tons of people spending money all of the time, regardless of what the economy is doing.

Let me break down for you exactly what I did and how I used the Law of Attraction to sky-rocket my success. I'll show you exactly how I went from making $300 a week to manifesting my dream of living in Hawaii, and later making $900 a day, all while getting paid to practice for a public-speaking career.

No. 1: ASK

Take the responsibility to see clearly what you want through contrast and create intentions.

If you haven't yet watched the hit movie The Secret, which explores the Law of Attraction, yet then do it!

The Law of Attraction states that like attracts like, meaning if you feel prosperous, prosperity must find you. Life is like a mirror. Your physical reality is nothing but an outer reflection of what you feel inside.

The Law does not discriminate. If you feel miserable, unworthy, unhappy, angry, unjustified, victimized, or sad, you cannot move into happiness, joy, or love.

This is how to feel your way to a better life "Law," and the good news is that no matter where you start – whether you're at the bottom of the barrel, broke like I was – you can start moving in the right direction toward wealth, abundance, prosperity, and joy.

"If you don't know what you want, you'll probably never get it."
– Jeffrey Gitomer

The first step in using the Law of Attraction is to know what you want. I notice it's easier for people to talk about what they don't like and what they don't want versus what they do want.

Take a few moments and grab a piece of paper. Jot down everything you hate about your life. Go ahead. I know this might sound absurd to you if you've studied the Law of Attraction before because it enforces focusing on what you do not want versus what you do want, but I promise you this is a very healthy exercise to get you in tune with your core wants. It also gets any stuck energy moving around areas in your life you want to see improvement in. Go ahead – grab a piece of paper and do this quick exercise.

Clarity equals speed in manifesting what you want, so don't skip this part!

Here is a sample chart to help give you some ideas.

What I Don't Want	What I Do Want	What I Don't Want to Feel	What I Do Want to Feel
I don't want to work at making someone else rich.	I want to work for myself.	I don't want to feel used.	I want to feel appreciated.
I don't want to work 40+ hours per week.	I want to be able to choose my hours depending on what's going on in my life that week.	I don't want to feel like I am owned, like I am a slave to the 9-to-5.	I want to feel free and in control of how I spend my time.
I don't want to work for people who are communicatively impaired.	I want to work with others who are able to easily and effectively communicate their ideas.	I don't want to feel disrespected.	I want to feel I am equal to my associates at work. I want to feel respected.
I don't want to sit in traffic half of my day to get to work.	I want to work close to home.	I don't want to feel rushed, panicked, and stressed all of the time.	I want to feel peaceful and relaxed.

I don't want to work at a monotonous, boring job.	I want to have a stimulating job that challenges me to progress and succeed.	I don't want to feel bored and useless.	I want to feel energetic, excited, and passionate about my work.

Got your list?

Congratulations!

Now that you've completed your want/don't want list, let me share with you how you will use it to create powerful intentions.

When you know what you want your energy becomes aligned instead of scattered – focused like a laser instead of spread out like a light bulb. The more in tune, aligned, and clear you are about what you want, the faster you can begin manifesting it. Clarity equals speed.

You see, life is always delivering crystal clarity for you about what you want by virtue of experiences that are showing up around you.

You see a brand new Mercedes convertible drive past you while you're in your beaten-up minivan and you say, "Hmm, I like that!"

When you have desire, it acts as rocket fuel for your intentions. Remember: Clarity always comes from contrast. So instead of looking at how crappy your life is, and focusing on the fact that you aren't making enough money or don't have nearly enough clients or enough confidence, you can always look at what is showing up and say, "Okay, now that I know what I don't want, what is it I do want?" Start there.

Now that you have more clarity about what it is you want, make a written intention.

My new intention was really clear:

> I want a job that will help me practice public speaking, pay me over $1,000 per week, be flexible, and allow me to travel, use and develop my talents, and, most importantly, let me live in Hawaii.

Those were my specific criteria. That was the intention I made after living in the Bronx and experiencing all of that struggle.

Two weeks later, I found the perfect job on Craigslist. The ad said: "Make $750 - $1,500 per week. Work part-time or full-time. Hiring actors to memorize a script and do live, in-store presentations. Work around your business or school and travel, even to Hawaii." I was sold!

That opportunity turned out to be my mop job.

I took the job, and two months later was on a plane to Hawaii, where I lived and worked (and played) for six months. I lived ten minutes from the beach! The Universe is so good.

Once I had the job, I used the same exercise as above to attract my ideal clients – and you can, too. Simply make a list of all of the character and personality traits you want your ideal clients to have.

Know what you want; be crystal clear. I know this sounds too simple, but sometimes the hardest things to do are the simplest things, so don't skip these exercises. Take the time to write them out. This helps you align your energy and lets the Universe know what it is you want.

Before doing her sales presentation, Melanie (in retail sales) rereads who her ideal clients are off of a list she keeps in her purse. "I have a little list on paper and I would reread my list just before to get myself in alignment with whom I want to interact."

Melanie's list goes something like this: "I want to be in my power. I want to be in balance. I want to connect with like-minded, happy, excited, fun people who love and adore me. I want to have fun and laugh, really laugh, and enjoy myself."

You can really have everything you want in life. You just have to know what it is and ask for it.

Here is what my ideal client list looks like.

My ideal clients:

- Have kids, pets, or grandkids.

- Are green and environmentally conscious.

- Want to save money.

- Think I am hilarious.

- Stay until the end of my show.

- Come running to my offers and are naturally curious people.

- Buy more than one– they buy 2 or 3 for family members as well.

- Really understand the value I am offering.
- Are fun, happy, excited people who add to the energy of the group.
- Listen well.
- Love my product and see the value in what I am doing.
- Have allergies.
- Love free gifts.
- Buy from me no matter what I say or how I say it.

Call to action: How can you pave your experiences to allow in more success, ease, and joy? Take some time right now to write down your want/don't want list and your ideal client profile list. Don't skip this process; it is very powerful! Clarity equals power and speed! What are your clients like? What kind of personality traits do they have? How do they treat you? How do you interact with them? How do they pay you? Do they refer you clients? Take some time and really get some clarity about who you want to do business with. Write this information down and watch these people show up without fail.

"When a person really desires something, the entire universe conspires to help that person realize his dream."

– *Paulo Coelho*

No. 2: BELIEVE

Reinforce by visualization, writing, and emotionally anchoring experiences in the body.

The second phase in the Law of Attraction is to believe that what you have asked for is on its way into your experience.

This is a very hard part for a lot of people. The most common complaints I hear are: "How can I focus on what I want when what I don't want is staring me in the face?" and "I've never had the experience of success before, so how do I know for sure I can create it?"

Doubt's a bitch.

It's normal for your ego to keep you from changing. Change, after all, is scary. It's uncertain, and means your little ego can't hold on to the same old familiar stories that keep you playing small.

Notice that when you feel doubt, resistance comes up about your new intentions. When you feel doubtful remind yourself that your thoughts create reality and that now you are choosing a new, more successful, prosperous, and abundant future for yourself.

Cultivating awareness about your emotions will let you know when you feel bad, when you feel off, upset, doubtful, nervous, and frustrated. The more time you spend emitting those emotions the longer it will take your new intention to manifest. The trick is to catch yourself when you feel off, restate your new intention, and then get into feeling good again.

I found the fastest way to manifest new intentions was to emotionally anchor them into my body.

Here is the exact exercise I used.

Visualization

Every night before bed I would lie down, close my eyes, and relax my body from head to toe.

Then I would imagine what life would be like in Hawaii: what the sun would feel like on my skin, the sand in my toes, the greenery around me, and the smell of the ocean.

I did this every night religiously. It took me maybe ten to twenty minutes. I would visualize what it would feel like to make $1,000 a week, what clothes I would wear, the restaurants I would eat at, etc.

The trick is, I would do this little visualization until I felt ripples or waves of energy go up and down my spine. I'm not a meditation expert or anything, but someone told me this is what the Yogis refer to as "kundalini" energy: the creative life force we all have that is released from the bottom of our spines.

Your mind cannot tell the difference between an imagined experience and a real experience.

When your body feels emotions it sends out those energy waves as vibrations that beckon back to you the subject of your intentions.

After reading *The Answer* by John Assaraf and Murray Smith I became aware of the scientific phenomena they call "neuro reconditioning," which is imprinting our subconscious through repetitive emotional patterning.

Imprinting these feelings over and over again each night before bed was creating new neuro pathways in my brain that allowed me attract to a fabulous experience living and working in Hawaii.

A neuro pathway is a connection – a firing of energy created through the repetition of emotion.

Creating a new neuro pathway is essentially creating new things for our brains to pay attention to as important. It's how we create beliefs.

You can decide to become a millionaire with your conscious mind, but if your subconscious mind believes you don't deserve wealth, then you're out of luck.

Your subconscious mind rules. It decides what action you take. So to change your life you have to find a way to change your beliefs.

That is how I did it. That's how I manifested a dream job in Hawaii. Religiously I relaxed my mind and body each night, and then visualized what it would feel like to actually live that dream.

The tricky part is to do it religiously! The more often you produce those feelings, the bigger the groove you create and the stronger the connection in the brain between the images you think and see and the feelings you produce.

You become a magnet, and all cooperative parts in the Universe start amassing. You can actually trick yourself by anchoring these emotions into your body. Take ten to twenty minutes a day to imagine yourself into the emotions of the success you want to have.

This takes discipline. The more disciplined you are to do this consistently, the faster your intentions will manifest!

"In essence, if we want to direct our lives, we must take control of our consistent actions. It's not what we do once in a while that shapes our lives, but what we do consistently."

– Tony Robbins

Call to action: Check out this free meditation I recorded (the very same meditation I did each night before bed) to help you get into the zone and help you manifest with ease and speed. Find the free download at www.TakeYourPowerBackNow.com/bonus.

Scripting

I also use a simple writing method called scripting that has profoundly changed my life.

In less than a year I tripled my income, bought a camper trailer to travel across Canada, wrote this book, and launched a new career using this fast, fun, and simple tool. It's very powerful, and I want to share with you just how easy it is to use.

Every morning I take twenty to thirty minutes to be present with myself and make some very precise intentions about exactly how much money I want to make that day and with whom I want to interact and have fun. I script out my day like an artist writes a script for a play.

Scripting can also be used to ask questions for answers you would like help with from your higher power, or subconscious mind. The simple task of asking for help starts your mind churning for answers, and pretty soon you will have those answers.

Here are three of my favorite ways to use scripting:

1. Write to connect for guidance and clarity from your higher power.
2. Make inner intentions for your outer reality experiences.
3. Just ask for help.

How Scripting Works

Let's say you're feeling a bit worried because you have a meeting at work today. You want to really communicate your ideas effectively, because the big cheese will be at this meeting, and your yearly evaluation is coming up soon. You need a raise, and you want to impress these people in your meeting today. Here's how you would script it into your day. Write what you want to happen for you. It might go something like this:

Help me communicate easily, effectively, and successfully today at the meeting so that I receive a huge bonus and pay raise this year.

Check how you feel inside. Is there more to it? Maybe you don't really believe you deserve a raise this year. Write that down, too. Ask for help.

Help me believe I deserve a 7% pay raise this year.

Check in: How do you feel? Is that it, or is there more to it? Maybe writing this down leads you to think that what you really want to do is make a lot more money and have way more free time to do the things you love to do instead of worrying for this company. So write it down.

Show me new opportunities for success where I can apply my talents, time, and energy in a new job/career that pays me $_____ per year and allows me to enjoy more free time. I want to work only 20 hours per week and make $_____. I want to enjoy the work that I do and feel passionate about it. I want to know I am really making a difference and serving the world from a place of total authenticity. I want to help people in a big way and feel appreciated for my time and efforts. Help me become aware of opportunities to serve and make a ton of money while having the most fun I've ever had!

You can see how scripting can be used for just about anything. You can use it for awakening awareness of new opportunities to feeling appreciated and even earning more money. Start by being present and feeling what is worrying you and what is bothering you.

Are you afraid of not being able to generate enough cash flow to pay the bills?

Are you worried you'll never figure out a good business to get into or find work that is truly fulfilling?

Maybe you want to attract a specific type of client, or are trying to decide whether or not to get a new job. Whatever is on your mind, take note if it.

Simply meet yourself where you are, and ask for what you want.

You will start seeing evidence of the Universe answering you shortly. Keep a record of the synchronicities – those "weird coincidences" that pop up to give you what it is you are wanting most.

Be open to answers from everywhere. Sometimes a question you have asked that morning will be answered by a stranger you hear in conversation passing you by in the street. Synchronicity is amazing; it's the magic and miraculous part of life!

Sample phrases you can use when scripting are:

I need major help and guidance...to figure out what career is best for me.

Someday, someway, somehow...I want to believe I can earn $800,000 per year.

Show me...exactly what to do to triple my income.

Help me...get really clear about what I'm offering my clients and help me find the perfect language to connect with them.

I am connected to spirit today...and I'm laughing till it hurts my cheeks!

Call to action: Get a journal and start scripting your new reality. Here are some questions to get you started: How much money do you want to earn this year? How much money do you want to earn today? What kind of work do you want to do? How would you like to feel on a daily basis? What would you like guidance on? From whom do you need support? This is a daily practice of compassion and self-love and the most amazing gift you can give to yourself. Try this for thirty days, and I promise the results will blow your socks off!

You can go to www.TakeYourPowerBackNow.com/bonus and print out a free PDF guide with a printable scripting workbook to get you started now. I created a bonus video about how to use scripting as well. Enjoy!

No. 3: RECEIVE

Allow it to materialize through feeling good and consistent gratitude.

"Honor yourself by always feeling good, because you really get a lot more done in less time and more easily when you come from a place of feeling good versus forcing and struggling to make it work for you."
— *Vanessa Simpkins*

No matter how hard you work, if you don't feel good first, if you don't take the time to cultivate a loving relationship with yourself and be good to yourself above everything else, all of your efforts will be in vain and failure will surely follow.

Forcing and pushing for productivity over honoring yourself and how you feel is from the old world paradigm of fear versus love.

Doing my mop shows, I'd start getting tired and hungry, I'd ache a bit in my legs, my voice would start cracking from screaming over the crowds on the weekends and, really, sometimes I just didn't feel like doing another show. But I would do one anyway.

What transpired time and time again is that I would blow the show or blank, and no one would buy after I'd spent fifteen to twenty-five minutes completely wasting my time. I was furious at myself!

Actually, I was furious at those poor, unsuspecting people in the store. At the time, I blamed them for being stale fish staring back at me with blank stares. It really wasn't their fault at all. I was the one who had no energy left.

People buy your energy, your presence, your power, and your expertise. They do not buy your products or services.

They buy your enthusiasm and contagious charisma about what it is you are selling. They buy how much fun you can have while selling. If you don't feel good to start with, you're a dead duck!

The trick to allow your intentions to materialize is to get into a good feeling space – find a way to feel good. Listen to what your body needs at this very moment. Do you need a rest? Are you thirsty? Do you need to go to the bathroom, but you're holding it in for one more sales call?

This sounds really simple, but, like I said before, simple is usually the hardest thing for people to grasp because it is right in front of their nose.

"At the heart of every desire is the desire to feel good. And so, the standard of success in life is not the things or the money; the standard of success is absolutely the amount of joy you feel."

– Esther Hicks

When you allow yourself to feel good, you connect back with the flow of creativity, you step into your full power presence, you enjoy the moment, you love yourself, and you radiate love. You also attract and allow your intentions to materialize, because your vibration is in high gear when you feel good and becomes a match to the vibration of what you have asked for.

The process is called allowing. Very tricky! Sounds easy, but remember that, if you are like the rest of us, you have also been programmed by society to struggle, push, force, and make things work for you.

Be careful. Your doubting mind will try to figure out "how" to bring about what you have asked for. The "how" is not your job; the "how" is the Universe's job. Figuring out the "what you want" is your job.

You must also be detached (not clinging or trying to make it happen). Doing, doing, doing in hopes that it will make it happen more quickly is not the way to succeed.

You must simply enjoy yourself and do what feels right. If you have a flash idea to make calls or meet someone or go for a drive or go get groceries, do that.

When you allow yourself to feel good your intuition kicks in. Listen to what it says. That small voice or gut feeling that whispers to call an old friend or visit your aunt in the nursing home might be completely unrelated to work, but listen to it.

The Universe works in magical ways to bring you what you want, but almost never in the ways you think it "should."

Don't beat yourself up if your intentions have not materialized by a certain time as you think they should have. Faith is knowing that the Universe works in divine timing and is always working in your best interest. Be gentle with yourself, give yourself a break, lie down and get some rest, eat some yummy food. Listen to your body, go outside and breathe some fresh air, and cultivate feeling good. This is an art! Pay attention to your thoughts and watch out for doubt creeping in. Commit to enjoying yourself. The more joy you have in life, the faster your intentions manifest!

Gratitude

A fast way to get to feeling good is to practice feeling grateful. I practice every morning in my gratitude journal. On one side of my journal I script my day and on the opposite page I write down what I am grateful for.

You can always choose to perceive the positive or negative side of life. Practicing gratitude is also creating a habit of focusing on what it is you want instead of falling on to complaints.

When you feel grateful, you automatically feel good and get into the flow of life. If you don't have a gratitude journal, get one. Start by writing down ten things you are grateful for each day. If you want more clients, start by being grateful for the ones you have.

Call to action: Schedule some time for feeling good this week. Maybe it's a pampering day at the spa or a night out on the town, a quiet bath and a good book, or laughing with a good friend. Whatever it is, if you find you aren't having enough fun in life, plan to go and have some! Get a gratitude journal or use your scripting journal, and combine both exercises like I do. Start by writing out ten things you are grateful for each day and expand from there. You will want to, because it feels so good! Print out your free gratitude journal PDF at www.TakeYourPowerBackNow.com/bonus

Chapter 4

The Inner Workings of a Masterful Salesman

Presence Is Power

Being present is the most important aspect of your sales success. When you are present you are tapped in, tuned in, and turned on to the flow of life. Make no mistake that this is what people buy: our powerful presence, out of which your authenticity is delivered loud and clear.

I talk a lot about presence, awareness, and authenticity in this book because when you are in your Full Power Presence, you have access to the essential energy that creates worlds, and people will pay you big money to witness, enjoy, and share in it with you.

Remember those moments when your life just worked, magically things clicked all of a sudden, and you felt unstoppable? When you allow yourself to exist in that space and maintain yourself in it, that's what I call stepping into your Full Power.

The problem is that if you are like most people, when you sell you aren't connected to that Full Power Presence. Most people have five million thoughts rushing through their brains (fear, doubt and worry distract them) and all of this can be felt unconsciously by their clients. To be good in sales you have to be present.

Being in my power meant the difference between selling $160 worth of mops and $1,000 worth of mops in just minutes!

Are you really present with your clients? Are you present in your daily activities as you run your business?

While selling mops in Sherbrooke, Quebec, I came across an interesting scenario. After one and then two great shows where no one bought, I asked myself, "What is going on here?" The frustration was building. Then I realized that I was competing with my audience. I tried to yell louder than the raucous ones who tried to distract the crowd with their antics, laughter, and funny jokes. Then I lost, of course, because I gave in to them. They got me every time I competed by raising my voice. I lost credibility, and I definitely did not maintain myself in my authenticity. I felt annoyed yelling at people, but I did it anyway, thinking that I had to compete. When I realized what I had been doing, I simply took a long, deep breath and shut up whenever people started to act up in the crowd, or I lowered my voice until it was barely audible, forcing the crowd to listen carefully if they wanted to hear me. I continued in a very quiet tone regardless of who was acting out.

This way, I maintained my authenticity. I didn't do anything I didn't want to do. I respected myself, I was present enough to know how I felt, and I acted from that space, not the space that is fraught with fear and says: "I have to yell to get their attention or they won't buy." This stems from competition. See the difference?

In truth, I have ruined shows several times by not being present and in my power. I've blown a presentation because I was over-analyzing it in my head; my thoughts were preoccupied, and my mind was running a million miles a minute. Or maybe someone was in a rush and I let him ruffle the crowd and ruffle me. I can't tell you how many times I have let this happen, until I realized what was really going on. It made me so mad! I was left thinking: "I've wasted my time! Rude, unappreciative people! I hate this job!"

The truth is, it was all my own fault. I went off, cooled down, and remembered who I was and what I was doing. I was sharing a wonderful product with the world: me. And I am totally amazing!

Sometimes you forget that, and that's okay. The important part is to remember who you really are and what you are here to do in this world.

We are powerful co-creators who often mistake our identities with the job we do, the clothes we wear, or the house we live in.

Don't beat yourself up if you slip. Remember: You are the one who is responsible for getting back to your Full Power Presence. Feeling rushed and feeling stressed are good indicators that you are not in your presence. Ask yourself, "Am I decorating my moment here? Am I in control of what I am doing? Am I letting outside circumstances dictate my behavior? Am I honoring how I feel above anything else. or am I acting from fear?"

Call to action: The best way to cultivate presence and awareness is by adopting a daily practice. I do yoga every day. I do just a bit, but it's enough to center myself and see how I am feeling. I have a stretch, feel good, and then get my day started. I also have my scripting and gratitude journal – this can also be a daily practice. Some people mediate; others go for a walk in nature. A daily practice is time away from everything else – a gift you give yourself to reflect on your life, what matters most to you, and to get centered balanced, strong, and confident instead of letting life blow you about with everyone else.

The Biggest Blocks to Your Success

You can try as hard as you like to be successful or more effective at sales, but as long as you have limiting programs drumming away all day long in your mind, your effort won't be long lasting.

Have you ever felt like no matter how hard you tried to be successful, something always happened to sabotage your success at the last minute? Maybe you've tried using the Law of Attraction before and have gotten poor results, or none at all. Maybe you've been able to enjoy some success but can't seem to break through to your end goal. Why are some things easy to manifest and others are seemingly impossible?

You have to understand how the mind works in order to effectively create change. Our conscious mind is the one with which we choose our thoughts. We consciously decide to use the Law of Attraction, for example. We consciously choose to improve our lives, get healthier, make more money, or take that vacation to Jamaica.

However, our subconscious mind is what really runs the show. Our subconscious beliefs are what create our reality. In an audio interview, Bruce Lipton, a cellular biologist and author, said something I will never forget: "...our subconscious mind is 1-million times more powerful than our conscious mind and is in operation 95% of the time."

If you're running around saying affirmations all day long, trying to be positive, and wondering why all of these other people out there are successful and you aren't, then it's time to realize you are fighting a very powerful machine! Your subconscious mind is only going to let you win 5% of the time – a very difficult feat to say the least!

In my coaching business, I notice that the biggest blocks with my clients involve perfectionism, feeling incompetent, a sense of deserving, worthiness, and a lack of trust in themselves and the Universe. Oh and the numero-uno trigger is always around the subject of money.

A client of mine, Dave, had a big "a-ha" one day during our coaching session. Dave is a highly creative engineer/inventor genius who has million-dollar ideas, but has been frustrated with trying to get his ideas launched and backed by investors. Dave was telling me how he was so sorry that he was late for our call. He was late for everything recently, racing around like a chicken with his head cut off. As we began talking, I asked Dave what the downside might be to becoming successful, if he did finally get everything he wanted with the right investors on board.

His answer: "I'm afraid I'll be so busy that I won't have time to be creative anymore."

That's the precise reason the investors he wanted couldn't find him. His beliefs were holding him out of their reach.

Here's another quick example of how simple beliefs affect your reality.

I was on vacation recently with my boyfriend, Dan, at the beach. We were on day two. Day one we spent lazing around and getting some rays, which was lovely. On day two, I thought to myself about how nice and how fun it would be to have a Frisbee like some of the kids did – to play around in the water and start moving a bit. That would be a lot of fun. I mentioned it to Dan. About forty-five minutes after

I had stated my intention to play with a Frisbee, we decided to take a walk down the beach. Two young guys walked right up to me and said, "Hey, would you guys like to have a Frisbee? We found a bunch of them just left here on the beach." Wow, that was so fast, and delivered right to us!

That was fine and dandy; a Frisbee is easy to manifest. We don't have any assumptions that state having too many Frisbees is evil or that you are a crook, a thief, or a bad person if you own too many Frisbees. I mean, God forbid you should have fun and have Frisbees falling into your experience from all over the place!

We aren't afraid that people won't love us if we have too many Frisbees or that people will only love us for our Frisbees and then we won't be able to tell if it's the Frisbee they love or us.

You get my point.

The Frisbee was easy to manifest – a perfect Law of Attraction delivery. Manifesting money, success, or growing your business to a certain level is often more difficult because of the stories you have around money and deserving success.

Again, these are all old programs that can be rewritten! That's the good news. You don't have to go through life with beliefs or programs that are of no more use to you: You can change them.

How do you shift from your limiting beliefs into beliefs that serve your vision of success? That is the million-dollar question!

Call to action: Ask yourself this question: "What is the downside to being successful and having everything I want?" Quickly write down the first answer that comes to mind even if it sounds ridiculous. This might surprise you!

How to Eliminate Self Sabotage and Self Limiting Beliefs

"See, the human mind is kind of like...a pinata. When it breaks open, there's a lot of surprises inside. Once you get the pinata perspective, you see that losing your mind can be a peak experience."

–Jane Wagner

When I was 20 and traveling in Asia, my trip brought me face-to-face with an 80-plus-year-old Chinese medical doctor in Beijing. Me, and a room full of eight or ten people, met with this old man who spoke no English and took our pulses, felt our thumbs, and looked at our tongues. Then, with stunning accuracy, he proceeded to diagnose each and every one of our aches, pains, and past illnesses (including my allergies from childhood and my friend's chronic indigestion).

That introduction to traditional Chinese medicine spurred me to study it myself under a fabulous acupuncturist named Anne St. Ammant. I later opened my own acupressure and massage therapy practice in Montreal.

The reason I'm telling you all of this is because my practice of Chinese medicine allowed me to thoroughly investigate how recurring thoughts and patterns of emotion affect the physical body in a very tangible way.

I love Chinese medicine because it is the science and study of how the mind, body, and spirit intertwine.

Did you know that anger and frustration harm your liver? What that means is that if you constantly let anger get the best of you, you may suffer from tension headaches and muscle aches all over your body. Because the liver is in charge of making the blood in the body, when its energy is depleted from anger, the liver can't give blood to the muscles. That is why you notice that a lot of people who suffer from fibromyalgia have outstanding anger issues.

Women with irregular menstrual cycles, with fibroids (stagnant blood), and many cases of depression are also linked to the emotion of anger/frustration and the liver. The liver plays a major role in making the blood, and the blood houses the "chi," or vital life force. If there isn't enough blood, there's not enough spirit – and there you have depression. You can't hide anything under the rug (or in your body). Your emotions play a huge role in your success; everything is related.

It is your responsibility to cultivate "feeling good" if you want to be an excellent salesperson. To feel good you've got to learn how to manage your emotions, because your thoughts create feelings, and feelings affect the physical body in a very big way.

Acupressure works with the energy meridians in the body, which are like passageways for the energy in our body – just like the electrical wiring for a house. You don't need to see the wires to know that when you turn on the light switch, the lights will go on.

My point is this: Acupressure works wonders to help people release the emotions stored in their physical body. There is an even quicker way to release these emotions, self-sabotaging beliefs, and patterns of defeating emotions that I absolutely love, love, love. I've used this method with fabulous success on my coaching clients, and it's called Emotional Freedom Technique, or EFT for short.

Call to action: The first step in releasing self-sabotaging beliefs is to cultivate an awareness of how you feel and what your emotions are telling you. In the next part of the book I'm going to share with you three simple and effective processes you can use immediately to eliminate self-sabotaging, limiting beliefs so you can move into lasting success once and for all.

Emotional Freedom Technique (EFT)

"All negative emotions are a result of a disruption in the body's energy system."

– Unknown

Emotional Freedom Technique is a very popular energy therapy that involves tapping certain points along the energy meridians on your body. It has grabbed the attention of some of the biggest names in medicine and personal development, such as Bob Proctor, Joe Vitale, Jack Canfield, and Dr. Norman Shealy, to name a few.

EFT has been used for years to help people with phobias and fears, dissipating them completely in sometimes as little as twenty minutes or less. EFT has worked wonders for people who suffer from addictions, poverty, allergies, deep-seated fears and phobias, pain, chronic illness, and more. The process is powerful and long-lasting. People have achieved amazing results in the arenas of limiting beliefs around money and self-worth as well.

I'm not going to go into a whole lot about it here in the book, as I find it's a whole lot more productive to participate in a tapping round so you feel the benefits. I have interviewed one of my favorite tapping experts, Brad Yates, and have included that interview for you as a bonus in this book.

This interview focuses on how to release negative assumptions about earning money in a lousy economy. You can try some tapping yourself. I'm sure you will love it!

Call to action: If you haven't already, go and download your bonus interview at www.TakeYourPowerBackNow.com/bonus.

Question Your Thoughts

"Who would you be without the thought...."

– Byron Katie

Another great tool I have used myself and with my clients is a process called "The Work." If you aren't familiar with Byron Katie, she is an author of three best-selling books, a workshop facilitator, and the inventor of a movement she has created called "The Work," which she teaches to millions of people around the world.

"The Work" teaches you how to end your own suffering through a simple process of questioning your thoughts.

Byron Katie has been on Oprah and has a fabulous personal story of triumph after suffering from major depression for several years. She developed a super-quick and simple process of self-inquiry that enables you to shift immediately from painful thoughts that hold you hostage to a shift in perception that brings instant relief. The process is called "The Work" and involves four questions you ask yourself to second-guess your thoughts.

It's when you believe you are your thoughts – when you attach yourself to your thoughts and believe that is who you are – that you suffer. The truth is you are much more powerful than your thoughts.

Call to action: Get the worksheets on Byron Katie's website (www. TheWork.com). They are free and downloadable. You can also access these sheets in the bonus section of this book at www.TakeYourPowerBackNow.com/bonus. Try it today! It's easy, simple, and fast for producing results. I love fast results! You can also access many of Byron Katie's videos on www.YouTube.com.

Ho opo nopono:
An Ancient Hawaiian Clearing Technique

"You can't get into 'enlightenment' without first releasing your 'black bags': your pain, anger, fear, unforgiveness."

– Unknown

Don't worry if you can't pronounce it properly; I have trouble pronouncing this myself. This simple breakthrough clearing process called Ho opo nopono, developed by Dr. Hu Lin, will blow your mind – in a good way, of course!

It is a simple process you can use in seconds to release the strongholds of your past conditioning, emotional trauma, subconscious fears, doubts, and worry that hold you back from success. As a sales professional, I have used this technique often while doing my shows because it allowed me to clear what needed clearing, even if I wasn't aware of what it was I was offering as resistance. You don't have to spend years in therapy to figure yourself out. Just do the process!

Again, I won't spend a ton of time explaining it because I interviewed Dr. Joe Vitale from the hit movie The Secret, and he describes how to use the technique in full depth. Lucky for you, I have also decided to include this audio recording for free with the accelerated workbook and transcription of the interview as part of the bonus with this book.

Call to action: Go to www.TakeYourPowerBackNow.com/bonus and download your free audio and transcript.

These are my favorite tools for reprogramming your subconscious mind for rock-solid sales success! Develop your inner mindset for success. It's a heck of a lot easier to work from the inside out and allow yourself to attract all of the people, resources, circumstances, and events you need to fulfill your intentions and mop up on cash with ease.

Chapter 5

The "Mop Up on Cash" System:

Nine Components of Selling Without Selling

Don't ever feel like you have to push, force, or manipulate your clients to buy from you ever again. If you really want to grow your business, make more money, and create a buying frenzy around your products and services (all while having more fun and being truly authentic) implement what I call the "Mop Up on Cash" system. This is a simple, nine-step formula I devised. If implemented correctly, it will help you sell without selling and turn your clients into raving fans who will want to come back and buy from you again and again.

1. Taste Test

"Ladies and gentlemen, in less than two minutes from right now we will start handing out brand new, FREE advertising gifts to each and every adult shopper in the store!"

– Vanessa Simpkins

Every great offer starts with a free gift. Whether it be a free report, free sample of your product, a free audio CD or a free consultation, a free goodie lets your audience "taste test" you to see if they want to move forward with you to the next level in the sales process.

Don't discredit how important this step is. Sometimes my clients tell me, "Oh, I don't know what to offer. There is so much out there already. Why would people buy from me?" The answer is, again, that people buy your energy. They buy your experience and your presence and expertise, so even if there are other similar products and services out there, some will want to learn from you.

Put your best foot forward and offer a free sample of some kind of no-risk offer that people can taste test you with.

During my sales shows in major department stores I would pick up the phone and make an announcement offering "free gifts to all of the adult shoppers in the store in less than two minutes," and you would be amazed at the crowds that showed up. People would be running and falling all over themselves to get these free gifts! I'm talking about high-class people in their fur coats. There is something in our psyche that gets set off when we hear the word free. Consciously we know better, but we can't help ourselves. We have to have it!

Here's a tip: Make a promise in your free gift. Make sure your free gift offers a catchy valuable promise. That way people will take you up on it and stay until the end of your offer, or read to the end of your free report, or listen until the end of your free audio. Promise one of the benefits. If you are selling a weight-loss program and your free sample is a milkshake, your promise could be: "Keeps you full for hours so you won't be hungry, and boosts your energy at the same time. Try it!" Add benefits as a promise in your free gift.

I told the people who arrived at the stage that there would be a "surprise" in a minute for those who kept a ticket in their hand. I said it was first come, first serve and that I couldn't do it for everyone, so they had to hold onto their ticket.

That promise of a surprise is what kept people around long enough to witness me demonstrate how amazing the product was. If I didn't make that promise, what do you think people would have done? Grabbed the free gift and ran, right?

The element of surprise is a commonly overlooked but highly effective technique to generate good feelings from your clients, and it helps you sell. Who doesn't love a surprise? In my case, promising the surprise served twofold purposes: It piqued their curiosity so they wanted to stay and see what it was, and by offering a surprise I over-delivered on value.

You want to also make your free taste test something of value that doesn't cost you much. It can even be a free download. Make it once and use it over and over again.

Your ability to excel in sales will be proportionate to your ability to create value even where there is little or no value. It's all about perceived value. I always say, give people something of value and much of that you will create.

The free gift we gave away at our shows was a lens cloth – a microfiber lens cloth, like you would get inside a case of fancy sunglasses. That's what I had to use to "wow" my clients. This was the taste test, and it worked beautifully.

Use it immediately! Be sure you create something your audience can use and ingest, read, or listen to. Make sure they can use it immediately! Don't make your free gift too big, too complicated, or too overwhelming. Instruct your audience to try, listen to, taste test your free gadget, report, or other immediately, because if not they will go on about their lives and forget. That's life. Use the opportunity to make sure to instruct your clients to use their free gift immediately.

My audience was convinced the microfiber worked because they tried it out on their glasses immediately. The other reason you want your audience to try it, listen to it, taste it, or use it immediately is because they will like it and then be more receptive and open to what else you have to offer. If I did a show and no one tried out the lens cloth first, I was just another pitch-y salesperson trying to sell them something they didn't need. When I was able to demonstrate the value of my product, they immediately opened up and started to trust me.

The purpose of the free gift is to get your prospects to know, like, and trust you.

Call to action: Get your free taste test in place. Create a free information product or a free report called "The Top 5 Mistakes ___ Make and How to Avoid Them." People love to know how they can avoid pain. Create an audio, get one of your friends to interview you about your business, and address your clients' top three or five problems and how you would solve them. Decide on a low-cost product to give out or a free fifteen- or twenty-minute consultation. Whatever it is, start offering your free gift to the world.

2. Be the Expert

"Learn to be difficult when it counts...having a reputation for being assertive will help you receive preferential treatment without having to beg or fight for it every time."

– Timothy Ferriss

People want to buy from an expert. As an expert, you offer people one very important thing: perspective. You are a knowledgeable expert. If you can teach your audience something they don't know while you sell, they will eat you up with a spoon.

Teaching while selling creates tremendous value for your clients. And while you educate, of course, you want to interject now and again the benefits your product or service delivers. Remember: Teach to sell.

Don't just jump into benefits right off the bat when speaking with people. You will sound like a cheesy car salesman if you do. Learn how to incorporate educational bits of information that your clients will take away with them. That way you will always stay in their minds as the one who provided the answer, the knowledge, and the solution.

The big problem I see with my coaching clients is that they think they have to be liked in order to sell. Sometimes you overdo it and then you just sound cheesy. Do you ever come across those kinds of salespeople? You just want to slap them, right? The truth is, people need to respect you in order to buy from you; they don't necessarily have to like you at all.

Be the expert they want to buy from. Look at Dr. Phil. He is abrasive and tells it like it is. He doesn't sugarcoat his message. It's raw and to the point, and sometimes he upsets people. But look at him: Thousands of people tune in every day to listen to Dr. Phil, the emotional expert in family matters.

Experts are controversial.

Many entrepreneurs starting out in business feel like they have to "be nice" to get the sale. On the contrary. You have to get your clients to respect you, and you do that by becoming the expert and teaching them. The faster you can teach your audience something, the faster they will trust you and recognize you as the expert, and the faster they will buy from you.

A good way to be seen as the expert is to diagnose their problem. Listen, then diagnose—just like a doctor. Remember: In sales, people don't care about your product; they really just want to feel understood.

If you do this properly you won't need to sell anything. People will be sold by your ability to diagnose them just like a professional does.

While selling the new microfiber mops, I pulled out the old stinky string mops and chemicals, and I reminded people it cost a lot of money to buy the refill products that pollute the environment— not to mention that people were ineffectively trying to clean their homes with these old smelly mops that were full of bacteria. I taught them a few facts and became an instant expert. I did this by making some bold statements and not caring if they liked what I had to say or not.

Remember that your job as a salesperson is to solve people's problems profitably. Most people won't have their problem at hand when they speak with you; it's your job to remind them. Otherwise they don't feel the pain, and they won't take action to buy.

You have to understand why people buy.

More people buy to overcome pain than any other reason.

Think about it: People buy more painkillers than vitamins. People buy for two reasons: to avoid pain and to gain pleasure (but more often to avoid pain).

Your job is to connect with them right away and let them know you understand their pain. Then half of your job is done! It has nothing to do with being nice and everything to do with being an expert.

One time I was working in Saskatchewan and I did a great show. Many people bought my mops. After the show was over, I was setting up the stage again and a couple came by. A lady who had watched the show brought her husband back with her to look at the mops. He started asking me questions: "So, how much is it?"

I told him it was $40. We kept chit-chatting, and again he asked me, "So, how much is it?"

I answered him again: "It's $40."

He and his wife were deciding if they should buy the mop, and I was busying myself with setting up more. Again the man asked me, "How much is it?"

I just couldn't help myself. I snapped back rudely without thinking, "What, are you deaf? I said it's 40 bucks!"

To my amazement, he bought it right then and there! He even bought a second mop for his brother, proving my point about being assertive.

What a mind-blowing concept. The truth is, if you're coming from your power and expertise and aren't afraid to lose the sale, then that's when you make it.

Call to action: Evaluate and change the way you communicate with your clients. Become the expert in "diagnosing" their pain and problems. What are five things you can teach your clients that they don't already know? Teach and share these tidbits of juicy info before talking sales, and you will never have to sell your product or service again. People will sell themselves on your expertise.

3. Stay in Your Power

"People buy personalities as much as merchandise and it is a question if they are not influenced more by the personalities with which they come in contact than they are by the merchandise."

– Napoleon Hill

Stand in your confidence and in your power and hold your own, because that is the authenticity that people buy.

I can't tell you the number of times I have blown a show because some wiseguy cracked a joke and then everyone laughed, including me, because it was funny. Then I lost control of the crowd and lost the sale.

Not only did I lose control of the crowd, but I gave the power to someone else and then lost credibility as well. Sometimes it was screaming kids or some announcement over the loudspeaker distracting the crowd. Regardless, if I didn't keep the control of the group and direct their attention, no sale resulted. People didn't understand the value of my product because they weren't paying attention and couldn't hear what I was saying.

There is a fine line between commanding attention and just being a control freak. No one buys from a control freak!

To be an expert in sales you have to be in control, and you do that by asking lots of questions.

When you ask questions you direct the flow of the conversation. I used many tricks to get people to refocus their attention on what I was saying. Sometimes, I varied my voice from a whisper to speaking loudly. Sometimes, I clapped my hands really loudly and snapped them back to attention, or flung the mop in the air so they would all turn and look at it, and I regained their attention. I had fun testing various methods.

If you lose control of the conversation, one way to get the ball back in your court is to ask lots of questions. Remember: People love to talk about themselves, so give them the chance.

If you speak more than you listen, and if you speak first without connecting and hearing the problem, you are instantly seen as a salesman. No one wants to buy from a salesman. People want to buy from an expert.

You also want to ask questions to get people to agree with you. When you can get people to agree with you, you start becoming hypnotic. I never realized it until recently when I was listening to Joe Vitale in an interview. He was talking about hypnotic marketing, and then it clicked. When I was on fire, the crowd was hypnotized – but not in a bad way. They were hanging off my every word! If you can get your audience (your clients) to pay attention to you and hang off your every word, your success is guaranteed.

This is so important because you train your clients how to react and treat you. My marketing mentor, Adam Urbanski, says, "Owning your own business is like owning your very own playground; it's your sandbox and if your clients don't play by your rules then throw 'em out!"

Don't be worried that you'll piss off a few people, either. Do you know how much time and energy you waste trying to please everyone? The truth is, you don't have to please everyone to make great money in sales or in business. Trying to please everyone is a surefire recipe for disaster. Some will buy, and some won't. Your goal is to get the right ones to work with you and buy from you.

Remember that sales is a numbers game. If I did a show and thirty people showed up, twenty-five would stay, and if I did a good job two-thirds would buy. Up your odds and stay in control. Remember who you're after. You are after clients you enjoy working and interacting with, and not everyone is an ideal client.

Stay in your power, be in control, and if some people are difficult with you then simply don't do business with them. Period. You'll save more energy for the people who will be the perfect fit. I'll get into how exactly to attract more of your ideal clients in a moment.

For now, remember that sales is a spiritual practice. You wouldn't start behaving in ways that don't feel right normally, so why start disrespecting yourself now in the sales process just for the promise of money? Be in control of yourself here, too, and don't do anything that doesn't feel good for you.

"I cannot give you the formula for success, but I can give you the formula for failure which is: Try to please everybody."

– Herbert B. Swope

Call to action: Practice taking the reins in your business. Answer the phone when it rings and tell people you are busy, even if it's a lie. Practice getting into the vibration – getting into the feeling of being a super success! You will be amazed at the new-found level of respect you command. You have to believe it and command it for yourself first.

4. Create Value: What's in it for Me?

"Try not to become a man of success but rather try to become a man of value."

– Albert Einstein

This is an ancient fact: People want to know what kind of benefit your product/service will do for them. Don't reinvent the wheel; just give it to them.

The problem I see with a lot of small business owners is that they try to sell the features of the product or service versus the benefits, and the truth is that no one really cares "how" your XYZ works.

People don't care what quality grade it has or how many grams of protein it has. They care about whether it will save them money or make them happier, sexier, slimmer, more lovable, healthier, etc.

You have to know exactly what you are selling.

When you speak your client's core language, speak to their triggers. Show them that you will create a lot of value for them.

Actually, there are only a handful of things people buy. Here they are listed (take note). People buy: security, sex, power, immortality, wealth, happiness, safety, health, recognition, and love – and not in that order.

Ask yourself if your sales message delivers these benefits. Ask yourself: How can I tailor your service or product to sell what people really want?

I'll let you in on a real secret here: I wasn't selling mops; I was selling vodka! Shh, don't tell anyone! Actually, I was selling a lifestyle.

You see, during my shows, I had a squirt bottle filled with water that I used to show people how they could easily clean by just using water. I got a mirror all gooey with Vaseline, hairspray, and toothpaste splashes, then I made a big joke about how I was using vodka to clean my mirrors.

People loved it. They thought it was a great joke. I realized what people were really buying was this carefree, easy lifestyle I portrayed – this image of cleaning the house while you drink vodka! Seriously, that's what they bought. Let's be honest here: The idea of cleaning your home is not fun!

People buy for emotional reasons first, and justify with logic and reason second.

Sometimes, after a huge show, there would be people holding the mop in their hands convincing other people around them why they needed it: "I've got kids and pets and a hairy husband. This is just what I need!" Or "I've been looking for something light-weight to clean my walls with. My husband smokes and the walls go yellow. This will be perfect!" And "I'm so tired of bending over and wringing out my old, stinky mop. I can't wait to go home and try it out!"

That's just the way it goes. People buy for emotional reasons, and justify with logic second. Don't try to reinvent the wheel here; you won't be changing brain patterns any time soon. So work with it, not against it.

How will your product or service satisfy your clients emotionally? Will it make their lives easier (people love easy), or will it help them save time or money? What is it?

You also want to show how your product or service bridges the gap between their problem and the solution. A great way to do this without telling them is to ask a question that, when they answer, will sell it for you. In essence, they sell themselves.

For example, on stage I had all sorts of toxic products that most people use to clean their homes. Before I told people the price of the mop (a much-higher price than your average $7 mop), I asked them all to raise their hands if they had three or more of those toxic products at home under their sinks. They all raised their hands; sometimes they raised both hands. Then I asked them how much they thought they spent on these products on a yearly basis, and they all moaned and groaned. It was a couple of hundred dollars at least – too much to count.

All I was doing was pointing out that it was money thrown in the garbage for nothing – money they could be saving by trying our product instead. Sold.

They sold themselves the moment they raised their hands and said "yes" to having more than three toxic products in their homes.

Become a master at over-delivering on value.

Give your clients more. Surprise them with an added goodie. After they agree to buy your product/service and it's a done deal, throw in something extra – something for free that they wouldn't think is coming. They will love you for it!

At the mop shows, I sold the mop and then added in a surprise at the end: a microfiber cleaning cloth worth $20 (but only if they bought my mop at that moment!). People were floored.

That little extra sealed the deal, and everyone walked away thinking they had just stumbled onto the next big thing since sliced bread. They got the deal of a lifetime!

How can you create that kind of feeling for your clients? You want to be known and remembered as a cool guy or gal who delivered incredible value, and at a steal.

Call to action: What are you really selling, and how are you tailoring your message to your clients so you add the benefits of what you are selling in your language? Looking back at this previous example. What are some types of "qualifying" questions you can ask your audience that will allow them to sell themselves without you having to sell? Are you over-delivering on value? Do you have another product or similar service you can offer your clients as a little bonus – as a way of sweetening your offer and delivering more value to them?

If you master these three steps outlined in this chapter properly you will never have to sell ever again. People will be asking you the big question – "How much?" – and that will take the selling part right out of the equation.

5. Compare Your Product or Service

"If you make people think they're thinking, they'll love you. If you really make them think, they'll hate you."

– Don Marquis

When you present your product or service, demonstrate how it compares to other products or services on the market. You'll answer their objections at the same time.

People are always on the lookout for a reasons not to buy – so don't give them one! Make it impossible for them to say no!

On stage, I had an old, cruddy, stinky mop to compare my mop with. I asked people to be honest and admit who had one of those "Mr. Stinky" mops hiding in their garage. Cue uproarious laughter. People thought it was hilarious! What they didn't realize was that psychologically they were all selling themselves on my product. Why? Because everyone else around them was in agreement that this old, stinky mop was horrendous and full of bacteria, and it smelled bad, and they were using it to clean their homes – not cool. They were all aware of their problem, and openly admitting it was a problem that they hadn't solved yet (drum roll please). Here comes the sale.

You always want to know your product or service well enough and be able to point out two or three benefits to using your "thing." You want to show how it's better at solving problems than anything that's already out there. This also adds credibility because it shows you know what you're talking about; you've been able to answer this question before because the answer rolls off your tongue.

You want to be able to stand out and offer your products and services as unique. If you're selling a service, what makes you the unique provider? What does your story say about you? If you're selling a product, how does it differ, and how is it better than what's already out there? Is it a price difference? Is it a convenience difference? Will it save people time or money?

Call to action: What do you need to know about similar products or services out there? What do you need to learn about your competition that will give you the ammunition of deciphering your unique abilities and differentiate you from everyone else out there? Get clear on how you or your service or product is different.

6. Testimonials + Social Proof

"It's been a thrill to watch Vanessa soar to top salesman in our company! As her manager, I can honestly say she is a pleasure to work with and a huge asset to our sales team. I have yet to meet anyone who could sell close to $6,000 a day worth of $40 mops! It always amazed me as I would watch Vanessa set her intentions for sales and hit her mark every time, and have tons and tons of fun bringing bright light to all who were around her. Congratulations on her ongoing success!"

Vanessa Mason, Market Manager of Retail Promotions,

You want to create the lure and show your clients that others who have purchased, or have done business with you in the past, have benefited from this interaction with you. You do this by showing social proof.

You see, no one wants to be the only one to buy or test you out. That isn't safe. People need to feel very safe in today's economy in order to buy. Remember that. Testimonials create a safe space – a safe environment to buy – because they show that others have previously taken the risk with you and enjoyed your product or service.

At the end of a show I asked for the sale. There was a bonus if people bought from the stage right then and there. I said: "But for those of you in this presentation who let me know right now," and I threw my hand in the air and asked them to raise their hands to let me know if they wanted one, "I'm going to give you this bonus for free inside your package today."

Sometimes, if I hadn't created enough value, people were hesitant to raise their hands, or they slightly raised their hands and looked around to see who else had their hands in the air. If no one raised their hands, I had to look far behind them and point to some fake person (who wasn't really there) and say, "You want one? Over there!" – when really, there was no one who was letting me know. Incredibly, people started raising their hands one by one to take the mop.

It's the psychology behind why people buy, and the truth is that people will buy when they know that they aren't the only ones. They will feel safe to buy when others have purchased and enjoyed your product or service already.

You want to make sure that on your website (if you have one) you have testimonials on your home page from people who have worked with you. Right away it gives you credibility and establishes your expertise.

Answering Objections with Testimonials and Stories

Another great tip I will share with you is to use stories as testimonials to overcome objections.

A story is a psychologically powerful sales tool. You might not think of it as such, but telling a story is often a very easy way for you to get your point across without sounding sales-y – a great habit to get into if you hate selling.

At the end of my shows, often people were hesitant to take the mop and pay for it at the cash register. They were unsure. Something I said or a way I behaved had all of sudden put them off. I hadn't been clear enough in telling them: "Here, take this mop and go pay over there."

People are like sheep: They need to be herded and gently nudged through a sales process in a way that feels good. They need to be led no matter what – actually, they expect to be led by you!

During a show, someone would ask me a question out loud, trying to decide if they really wanted to purchase this mop after the show. They had the mop in hand, but were hesitant all of a sudden. And instead of telling them "Yes, it's a great mop," or answering the question again, going over what I had said during my show, I told a story to demonstrate my point.

What I realized is that if I just told them the answer to a question they already knew two things would occur:

If I repeated myself in answering an obvious question I had already covered, I was discrediting myself by reselling after the show was over. A good salesman doesn't need to sell twice to the same person.

I realized they weren't asking the question because they wanted the factual answer. What they wanted was reassurance that they were making the right decision in purchasing this mop.

For example, if a woman asked me if she needed to use products with the mop (a really dumb question, considering the entire presentation is about how you don't need to use chemicals with this mop) instead of answering "no" I would tell her this story:

"You know, my aunt uses this mop. She has two cottages that she rents out and cleans every week. She was very skeptical about this mop because she loves her products. Anyway, I gave her one for Christmas a few years back so she could try it out. She called me the next day and raved on and on about how great it was. She told me to get her two more (one for each cottage and one for her house in the city)!"

Sold. What I had just done was answer the skeptical client's un-asked questions. She wasn't asking me if the mop would work without chemicals. She was skeptical. Obviously, my convincing, persuasive, and fun show wasn't enough to get her to buy. What I did was tell her a story that involved a third person: my aunt. My aunt was just like her – skeptical – and she had loved the mop.

Using stories to overcome objections in sales is powerful! It creates a third-party testimonial. This gives your clients what they really want: the feeling of being safe to take this next step with you in the sales process.

Call to action: Send out an e-mail to your clients and ask for testimonials. Do it right now. Put down the book, jump on the computer if you can, and send that e-mail. Simply ask for testimonials if you don't have any of your own, and even offer to write them with the person over the phone together. If you have testimonials and aren't putting them to good use, then what are you waiting for? Set some time aside right now to come up with an analogy or a few quick stories that answer your clients' FAQs and give third-person credibility and social proof.

"For the short amount of time Vanessa spent in our store in the fall, she hit consistently high sales volume every day that she was there. I was astounded at the amount that she sold and the delight she brought to those she was selling to! I've been working with this company for 38 years and it takes a lot to amaze me! Vanessa, you are truly amazing!"
– Larry Randall, Sears Store Manager

I just couldn't resist putting another one in here. :)

7. Guarantees

"The average man does not want to be free. He simply wants to be safe."
– H. L. Mencken

Most people don't really understand sales. A sale is, again, an exchange of energy where you solve people's problems profitably and make it easy for people to feel good about their decision.

People love to buy, but hate to be sold to.

If you can make it easy for them to buy, the sale is halfway done.

That's where guarantees come in. A guarantee ensures that people won't lose out if they try your offer. People hate to lose, and there are so many scams out there that the majority of people are really skeptical about anything they have to pay for – unless they get referred to you, of course.

So, offer a guarantee that will allow them to buy and feel good about taking a step forward without losing in any way. Make it easy for them to feel good about doing business with you.

That guarantees the sale.

I really have to commend the people at this company for their sales script because it is flawless – well, almost flawless. It is so well done. I'm sure thousands of dollars were spent perfecting this script that the company gives to its agents to memorize in order to sell their products. It is so effective! The script highlights guarantees.

If ever I skipped over the guarantees, or went over them too quickly, less people would buy. What I did was talk about the product's guarantees and look at people in the eye. I got them to agree with me that it was a no-risk offer. If they didn't like the product, they could come back to the store within ninety days and get a refund – no questions asked. Even if they tried the product and didn't like it, it didn't matter; they had a ninety-day satisfaction guarantee.

Often, a guarantee is the last part of the equation that people need in order to buy. You can always justify a price for your product. As long as you have a good guarantee people will feel safe enough to buy it.

This is very important. Make sure your offer includes a guarantee.

Without it your business will suffer. And make it a 100% satisfaction or money-back guarantee. Anything less just won't cut it.

Don't be afraid that you might lose out by offering solid guarantees, or that people will take advantage of you because of them. The truth is, there will always be some people who will take advantage of you and your offer – you can expect it to happen. However, the number of people you will be able to persuade to buy because of your spectacular guarantee will greatly outweigh the small number of those who try and take advantage of you. Offering money-back guarantees in your business is a must.

Call to action: If you don't already offer some type of guarantee in your business, get to it! Keep in mind that the higher the asking price of your product or service, the better the guarantee you should offer.

8. Create a Call to Action and the Urgency to Buy NOW!

"The world is a dangerous place, not because of those who do evil, but because of those who look on and do nothing."

– Albert Einstein

Call to ACTION!

Know when you have come to the end of your presentation, and know how to ask for the sale with a clear "**call to action**." This might sound obvious, but don't laugh. Some people think that once they are done talking and presenting, they won't have to ask for the sale. Wrong. Remember: People like to follow the leader. While you're selling, you are the leader.

Oftentimes people won't say "I want it" – not because they don't want it, but because they are being polite and waiting for you to ask for the sale. You don't ask because you don't want to sound pushy.

Spell it out for them: Tell your prospects what to do next. "Click here" for example; "fill out this form"; "I'm going to pass your credit card"; "pay over there"; etc.

While selling mops at the end of my presentation I said, "Okay. Everyone raise your hands. This is what you're going to get...."

It doesn't get more straightforward than that.

You want to make it clear to people what to do next. If they want it, they'll go for it or they will ask you more questions, which simply means you have neglected to deliver enough value, and that is what's preventing them from feeling good about taking the next step with you.

Often, after a show was finished and I'd handed out all of my mops, people stood there, milling around in front of the stage. I had to tell them: "Take this and pay for it at the cash register, now. There's a cash register over there. Go there and pay for it." Don't assume people know what you want them to do. Spell it out for them. Make it easy; you'll make more money that way!

Urgency

Always make a bonus for people as an incentive to buy from you now. People love to get a great deal. Think back to the last time you went shopping and came across a great deal on a shirt that you still wear and still talk about to your friends to this day! That's the kind of experience you want to create for your clients. You want to give them the "Oh, my God – what a great deal! Of course I want it!" feeling.

You want to make your bonus time-special, like "today only" or "for the next four days." You want to create a sense of urgency by letting people know you will give them a special bonus or help them save some money if they buy right now.

People buy out of fear of loss or greed, and more people buy from fear of loss.

The truth is, all of my presentations were based on this principle. I did a show and presented the value of the mop or product, and people loved it. They sold themselves on it, and waited for the price. They heard the guarantee, the price, the offer at a discount today, and then (if they let me know right then) the bonus.

Now, if I did my job properly, people were already sold on the mop at a discounted price. Great news! Adding the special bonus – that surprise that I promised from the beginning – the first-come-first-serve surprise that I couldn't do for everyone in the store (fear of loss) – swayed the people who were still on the fence about buying and got them to raise their hands and take one right away.

Offering a special bonus also wins you points by helping you make people think they are special! People love to feel special. Offering a time-based bonus or limited-quantity bonus adds some scarcity and will help you triple – even quadruple – your sales volume.

I know you might be thinking, "Ick. Too sales-y. I can't do it! I won't do it!"

Remember why people buy. They buy to avoid pain over gaining pleasure. And losing out on a great deal and suffering the pain of regret are very powerful.

Call to action: Are you leading your clients to the action you want them to take easily, smoothly, and directly? Do you ask for the sale? Do you hesitate when it comes time to ask for the money? Is your offer clear? Do you offer a bonus or do regular promotions to get your clients to take action now?

9. Keep Asking!

"If you want to be successful in life, learn how to ask for and get what you want. That is success in a nutshell."

– Vanessa Simpkins

This is where salespeople flounder. You ask for the sale once and if you don't get a favourable answer – an excited "yes" – you creep into a hole and die.

This is an interesting dynamic of human psychology. I played around with this.

Let's say I was at the end of my show and it was time for my clients to raise their hands and grab a mop, but no one raised their hands. Obviously I didn't add enough value to the offer, or make it juicy enough for them to take action. They were all standing there with blank faces staring back at me. I stood in my power and repeated, and repeated, and repeated, and kept asking until one brave soul took one. Then the rest of them reached forward and grabbed one, too.

There are two things going on here: First, like I've said several times, people buy your confidence and energy. Nothing screams confidence louder than the ability to ask, and ask, and ask for what you want.

"What they really purchase is the pleasing personality of some man or woman who knows the value of cultivating such a personality."
— Napoleon Hill

Subconsciously, when you ask for the sale again and again this says: "Hey, my thing rocks and I know you're going to think it rocks, too. So what are you waiting for?" It puts the attention back on them, and makes them feel like there is something wrong with them if they don't buy. Of course, there is if they have stayed and listened to you all that time without buying, right? If they weren't interested, they wouldn't have stayed and listened to your presentation.

Whether it's in your e-mail follow-up if you sell your products and services on-line or in person, you want to continue asking for the sale a few times. Especially if you're selling on-line, sometimes people just don't get your first or second e-mail. Life is busy. Don't assume that people are paying attention to you either when you ask. They might have their head in the clouds.

When one person sees someone else wanting something, enjoying something, and seeing its value, it allows them permission to do the same and not think they are the only ones. People are like sheep: They all follow each other. That's why having testimonials are so important.

Whether it's in your sales copy or in your presentation, ask again and again. If it's your fault and you didn't create enough value, you will know, because your clients will ask questions and have objections that they need clarification from you.

I know that asking for the sale is a bit counter-intuitive to sell without selling. I include it here because having the courage to ask again and again if your clients haven't already bought from you gets the buyers' objections out for you to hear.

Sometimes, your prospects won't tell you the truth about why they don't want to buy. By asking for the sale again and again, they will eventually get to the real reason that's preventing them from buying.

Chapter Takeaways:

This makes up my nine-step formula for rock-solid sales to help you sell without having to sell or sound pushy or sales-y. I suggest you get cooking and start implementing these techniques in your business or sales process today. I guarantee that if you follow this recipe you won't believe how easy it is to sell, because you will have allowed people to sell themselves on you first!

Call to action: Go over the "Mop Up on Cash" system with its nine steps to sell without selling, and make sure you implement these nine steps as part of your sales process:

1) Taste Test
2) Be the Expert
3) Stay in Your Power
4) Create Value: What's in it for Me?
5) Compare Your Product or Service
6) Testimonials + Social Proof
7) Guarantees
8) Create a **Call to Action** and the Urgency to Buy NOW
9) Keep Asking

Chapter 6

The Biggest-Kept Secret: How to Sell without Selling

"People rarely succeed unless they have fun in what they are doing."
– Dale Carnegie

Have fun. That's your goal!

Have fun when you're selling. It takes the pressure off of selling and you win no matter what, because you're enjoying yourself, you're present, you have energy, and you're not offering needy resistance. By having fun you send out the vibration, knowing and trusting that what you have asked is on its way. So the perfect clients will show up and buy.

This is a tricky balance because you don't want to have too much fun and then ruin your credibility; this really depends on what product or service you are selling. Selling bio-friendly mops is a bit of a serious matter compared to life coaching people selling balance and happiness, right? Then you'd want to really let loose and have fun, because fun is what your clients are buying.

Mostly, having fun creates the allure of confidence. Some of the best salesmen crack jokes left, right, and center and you wonder, "Jeez, they make it look like so much fun. It looks so easy." Well, it is. People buy this confidence. I've said this over and over in this book, but it really is the foundation of a fabulous salesperson: the ability to create confidence, fun, and ease with people.I came back from a small weekend conference of about seventy-five people in Ottawa, and the speaker started his workshop with pictures of himself naked in a tree, wearing only a loin cloth. You wouldn't expect this from a respected professional who has a master's degree in forestry. His introduction was absolutely hilarious, and before long the entire room was in an uproar. He made fun of himself and showed the room that he was there to have fun above everything else. Guess what happened during the break? There was no hard selling involved. Everyone was lined up in the back of the room to buy his books and DVDs by the armful –including me.

Having fun while you are selling is sometimes the missing piece you need to unlock your mega bucks. It's the one little tweak you can make in an instant that will shift your sales numbers into high gear. Having fun means you are confident enough to enjoy yourself, and it sends a message to the Universe that says: "Making money is easy."

When you smile, laugh, and crack jokes you deliver humor, and humor naturally allows you to connect easily with people – no matter who you are speaking with. By introducing humor you let your audience know you are human, too.

When people came to the mop stage and huddled around me, waiting expectantly, most of them were very sceptical and weary of me, standing there with their arms folded. I simply asked them, "So, you guys excited or just curious?" This would break the ice. People laughed at themselves because they noticed how tense they were. As soon as the ice was broken everyone relaxed and enjoyed themselves.

Having fun while selling is the biggest-kept secret to my sales success. At a company I sell mops for, what I do is called "retail-tainment" – and for a good reason.

Call to action: Are you being too stiff and too serious with your clients? How can you add more fun into your sales process? Research a few good jokes and memorize them, have them ready to go, and throw them in when you feel like it. Having fun is the secret clincher that closes a sale every time.

Let Go, Relax, and Receive

"Any and all desires can be fulfilled unless you are holding yourself out of alignment with your own desire. The feeling of competition or shortage, or limitation of resources, means you are out of alignment with you own desire."

– Esther Hicks and Abraham

If I was worried that people wouldn't buy my mops or if it was a quiet day in the store with not many clients around, and I thought, "I really need these people to buy my mops now," then no one bought. People can feel desperation. You can sense this; you can feel when someone is selling you and when someone is needy.

The Universe can't buy into your decision to want and attract something better, because you are giving it the opposite command with thoughts of lack.

My uncle went out and bought himself a "Big Green Egg," which is a very popular slow-cooking kind of sealed ceramic BBQ that sells for over $1,000. My uncle went into the store and decided that that day was the day to purchase this Big Green Egg and was approached by an older salesman.

He asked the salesman questions about what size to get, and the salesman simply agreed with everything my uncle said without really offering any expertise to advise him. This is the Old World sales model where you can feel the desperation that this salesperson had: No matter what, he just wanted to sell the "egg."

That day, the salesman lost his sale. My uncle didn't buy from him. He went home and bought his Big Green Egg by telephone and had it delivered. He didn't want to buy from someone who was just interested in the sale.

How do you detach and let go from the outcome of the sale, and just relax, have fun. and be present? How do you have faith that what you want is on its way? The allowing part of this is the hardest part in using the Law of Attraction.

Ask, Believe, Receive: this is the receiving part of it and the part most people have so much trouble with. So, I thought I would add a bit more here.

This really ties into to treating selling as a spiritual practice. Any time you find yourself forcing, struggling, or trying to make something happen to no avail, and the world seems like it's coming down on you, you have to stop. Simply stop what you're doing and go get some fresh air. Take a break.

We have been programmed to suffer and struggle for success. Instead, allow success in. This is a completely new paradigm.

I'm not saying you shouldn't work hard, because you have to take action. What I am saying is that when things are frustrating you to no end, don't keep forcing them anymore.

It's time to detach and stop pushing to make things happen your way. There is probably a better idea on its way, or a better way to accomplish something that you haven't thought of yet because you've been too busy forcing things to turn out the way you want them to.

When you force, you offer resistance. When you enjoy yourself, you tell the Universe: "Hey, I'm easygoing. I know that what I want is on its way. I can relax and let go and have fun." Before you know it, the subject of your desire shows up.

Whenever you feel at your wit's end (like nothing is going your way), that's the time to detach, let go, and do something completely different. Go for a coffee break or, if you can, take a day off and don't do any work. Go and have fun; get out into nature; relax.

Take some paper and a pen with you because you are going to need them. Once you let go it's just amazing how many ideas pop into your mind that you hadn't thought of before because you aren't offering resistance by trying to figure things out.

Call to action: If you've done your inner and outer work, get ready to receive. What can you do to let go, relax, and enjoy yourself "in the meantime" until your desire manifests? What actions can you take right now that will send out the vibration of "expectancy" that your abundance is on its way? The best way to say to the Universe that you expect it to manifest is to have fun. So plan in some "me" time and go have fun.

Connecting with Your Inner Guidance

"The intuitive mind is a sacred gift and the rational mind is a faithful servant. We have created a society that honours the servant and has forgotten the gift."

– Albert Einstein

Selling is very empathetic. It is a very feeling-oriented business. Interestingly enough, the best salespeople have developed their intuition and can feel clients' concerns and questions even before they ask them.

Every great leader – and as a salesperson you are the leader – has fine-tuned this ability to follow his or her intuition or inner guidance. It's this intuitive nudge to ask the right questions or "feel" his or her way through the sales process and just know the right time to close the deal.

That's why cultivating a strong connection with your inner guidance is so important, and doing just this alone will help you in so many areas of your life (personal and, of course, your work), as your business is just an extension of yourself.

The problem is that connecting with your inner guidance or intuition isn't something they teach you in school – at least not in the mainstream education system. They also don't teach you how to cultivate healthy relationships, be happy, make money, or shop for a mortgage. It's your job to figure out exactly how to connect and receive this guidance from your inner being because it will tell you exactly what action to take that will lead you down your path of success, abundance, and rock-solid sales.

How can you tell you are listening to your intuition and not the voice of your ego?

Good question.

Intuition feels like a hunch, an inner nudge, or just a faint desire to go check something out, watch something, or call someone. Intuition directs you in many ways which might include sometimes just stopping, sitting down, and relaxing. Most often we don't listen, right? We just keep plowing forward: busy, busy, no time to reflect, sit, and be quiet.

The ego will lead you into feeling superior, better than others, aggressive, defensive, or "off," meaning not feeling good. It is a false power.

The first step in tuning in with your inner guidance or intuition is to just be still and quiet. Close your eyes, breathe, and listen. Then do what feels right for you.

A woman I admire a lot, Marci Lebowitz, coaches her clients to tune in to their inner guidance. She helps frustrated souls discover their life's work. Her sales process is unique and unlike anything I have ever seen before. She consults with new clients and then urges them to sit with her and receive guidance over the next few days to see if they are really a good match to work together. Right from the start, Marci is teaching her clients to rely on their own inner guidance for the answers they seek.

Taking action from a place of inspiration instead of fear will transform your life in truly unimaginable ways.

Honor yourself and love yourself enough to listen to your own voice of reason – your inner guidance; it will always lead you onto your next step in life.

In business, having this "sixth" sense can go a long way not only in helping you close more sales by being more present, focused, and tuned in to your clients needs, but it will also help you decipher ideal business partners, investors, clients, etc.

Sometimes you just know when it's right to pick up the phone and call on someone; you get a flash in your mind about them. Or you have a nagging feeling that won't let you go, so you drive out to visit someone, and the most amazing turn of events transpires.

I believe you were born with an innate set of "lessons" you were meant to learn here on Earth. There are people who are here to help you on your path – things that you are meant to do. It's by following your intuition (some people call it "following your bliss") – this good feeling – that will always lead you in the right direction.

"To be yourself in a world that is constantly trying to make you something else is the greatest accomplishment."

— *Ralph Waldo Emerson*

Once you connect with your voice of intuition, you never forget how to do it. You might choose to forget for a while, and then get back in tune and continue your journey. If you can learn to follow your guidance, you will be amazed at the synchronicities and wonderful ways life delivers your requests as if by magic.

Most of all, you will always find a way to get the answers to your most burning questions, and you will feel supported and loved in a whole new light.

Call to action: If you are unsure about what to do and have anxiety about a certain subject, stop and remember to ask for guidance. Ask for the ability to hear, connect with, develop, and receive guidance from your intuition or higher self. You can even write for it using your scripting process (download your PDF version on the bonus page found at www.TakeYourPowerBackNow.com/bonus). Get ready for some mind-blowing synchronicity to show up in your life.

Chapter 7

Connecting with the Abundance and Power in Nature

"I love to think of nature as an unlimited broadcasting station, through which God speaks to us every hour, if we will only tune in."
                                                    – George Washington Carver

My personal secret to success, and something my dad taught me early on is that "nature is where it's really at."

My father's life was a tribute to nature. He painted wonderful fields full of colorful flowers, rolling blue mountains, pink lilies in ponds, and endless skies filled with white, puffy clouds.

Interestingly, my father, who was this eccentric artist – someone who never fit into society – didn't buy into the system, and he was totally void of any kind of materialistic bone in his entire body. He was someone who lived life on his own terms and in his own way – even if it pissed some people off. Interestingly enough, my father's clients who purchased his natural landscape paintings were all high-powered executives, judges, lawyers, and pharmaceutical reps. They were people who had given up that connection with nature to pursue the financial security of the corporate world. My father's work put back that connection with nature.

I realized that they were buying freedom from my dad. His paintings were a testament to his lifestyle. He'd go out and work (meaning he'd venture off into the wild, find a space that intrigued him, called to him, or spoke to him, and spend his afternoon immersed in the scene, in the stunningly beautiful feeling that nature inspired in him) and then he happily paint away, tapping into the creative flow of life. Remember: My father was a happy guy who died with a smile on his face.

I believe that the way one dies speaks volumes about the way one lives.

The biggest problem with modern society is that it completely distracts and disconnects us from nature and our source. The human body, after all, is an electrical field with energy coursing through it. The same is true with living plants and trees. You can't recharge your batteries by sitting in front of the TV or shopping in a mall. Energy comes from direct contact and connections with the source that created us: nature.

Recently, I was out at my favorite spot close to home. In the mountains off a nearby bike trail, there is a wonderful river with small falls and cool water that is simply divine. I took the afternoon off to celebrate my friend Anita's birthday. We brought along her dog, a picnic, and our bathing suits.

For weeks I was unable to decide where my next mop venture would be. In sort of a panic, work called me over one week before that day to get my commitment for my next store, and I just couldn't decide. I couldn't feel what the next step was. Basically, I was confused.

During that afternoon, while at the magical spot in nature lolling about and enjoying the sun, magically my manager called me and offered me the perfect location to work.

As we were packing up to leave the river a guy who was there with his dog asked us if we had lost a chain and showed us a beautiful silver necklace he'd found on the shore.

"No," I said. "It's not mine, but it sure is lovely!"

"Take it," he said. "It's yours."

I was floored! Just the day before I was looking at my jewelry and saying to myself that I needed to buy a nice silver chain, and a day later it was delivered to me.

The experience of immersing yourself in nature proves twofold. First you re-connect and recharge, and second you let go and relax. This allows you to feel great, but also switches off that "trying, trying, trying" mechanism. You know that "have to be doing something all of the time" mode that actually causes more stress, delivers more resistance, and forces energy instead of effectively and easily allowing energy.

Isn't' it true that your biggest "a-ha!" moments often come when you are connected and immersed in nature, while walking on the beach or in the forest enjoying the sunshine and natural beauty that surround you?

When you relax and enjoy God's creations, you allow the magic to unfold before your eyes. It takes a trust in faith that you can allow yourself the pleasure of really unwinding and letting go. By doing this you actually become much more productive.

You know how peaceful, centered, calm, and rejuvenated you feel after a vacation at the beach, swimming in the ocean, or at a cottage by the lake. Imagine what a super success you would be if you brought that calm, centered, balanced, focused feeling to your job or your business every day.

Nature Is Full of Abundance

Have you ever sat by a lake and wondered how many droplets of water it takes to fill it? Or looked over the landscape at all of the millions of trees and wondered how many leaves are on each one, or how many pine needles are on one tree?

Nature has it all – abundance galore! Any time you feel out of sorts or fall into stinking thinking or a scarcity mentality, get out into nature. The experience will rejuvenate you and remind you of what you really are: an extension of this abundant force of life.

I believe that, living in cities, we've become too far removed from our origin – from the abundant, wise, and supportive nature we belong to. We've been so brainwashed to adopt other people's style of life, beliefs, and ideals that we've forgotten how to honor what is right for the individual – ourselves.

There is an internal knowing – access to ancient wisdom – that we can all tap into only we are so cut off from this information (living in a fast-paced society with no time, no peace, no quiet, no rustling wind, no living things; with everything replaced with fake, material-istic things).

Nature brings you back to your authentic self. It fills you up with energy and reconnects you to the bigger picture. Any time you feel off-beat, get outside, take a walk, and go out and explore the wonder, simplicity, and abundance all around you. It is the quickest, surest way to reconnect with you and your authenticity, your presence, your awareness, stillness, peace, and love that are naturally made to radiate from the core of your being.

"Forget not that the earth delights to feel your bare feet and the winds long to play with your hair."

– Kahlil Gibran

Call to action: Plan regular retreats in nature, whether it be your own outdoor adventure, an afternoon hike, or a mini three-day vaca-tion to someplace cool – somewhere you've always wanted to go but have never "had the time" to see. Plan it into your schedule within the next two weeks. Practice becoming more aware of the simple beauty, the fresh air, and the peace and quiet nature affords you. After all, it's free!

Chapter 8

Bringing it All Together

Sales as a spiritual practice is just like the journey to lasting wealth and freedom. It is the very same journey you take to reach your authentic self. You can gain clarity by looking at what is showing up in your business or by looking at the results you are getting from selling your products and services.

Cultivate personal responsibility and awareness for how you feel first and foremost.

Question yourself. Ask what sabotages your ability to be authentic, true, and present with others. Learn to be present, to slow down, to listen, and to honor the voice within.

How can you become a bright, shiny light that draws in all of the opportunities, clients, circumstances, and support that you need with ease and speed?

Remember that life is like a mirror. You have to clean the surface to see clearly the reflection of what you want. When you clean and clear you won't have to force and push to get what you want. You will open the gateway to the path of least resistance and allow a direct path to reach you for what you are wanting.

Use the Law of Attraction in your personal life, and watch it transform and transfer to your business life. Ask, Believe, Receive. Get into the rhythm of a habitual daily practice of felling good no matter what, in every situation, until it becomes second nature.

Commit to imprinting your new emotional patterns onto the subconscious, do your nightly meditations, and watch your life transform!

Remember to drop the social conditioning of what is acceptable behavior in business. Authenticity is what sells. Period.

You have to be responsible and reprogram your vision of success. Use the tools for emotional release work so you can be present in the power of now.

Being present and authentic in every moment of your day, especially while you are in the process of engaging in your sales process, will determine your success. Halt the assumptions that keep you away from abundance and prosperity – the money blocks and the limiting beliefs that keep you away from enjoying the freedom of wealth.

Mastering sales is really creating an irresistible offer that over-delivers value to people. You can use the "Mop Up on Cash" system outlined in this book. Make sure you incorporate all nine components to your special offer, and selling will never feel like selling again.

Ask yourself: "How can I create something of real value for my clients?" Focus on that versus outshining your competitors. When you ask a question, your mind immediately tries to find the answer for you.

Learn to have more fun and your success will come that much faster. Make your intentions, take actions, and then detach from the outcome. The easiest way to tell the Universe that you have faith that all is on its way is to have fun.

Allow yourself to enjoy life more. Life is short, so you may as well enjoy it. Some people have this idea that to be in business is serious. This is defiantly simple and often the hardest part about achieving lasting success. Don't get caught up in feeling guilty for enjoying yourself and treating yourself with respect and kindness.

Most importantly, connect with nature so you become tuned in to the abundance of nature, and get back to your roots and the unique bites of wisdom that reside in us. You'll activate your energy when you immerse yourself in the divine creation.

Grow a garden. Plant something. Create a space of love on your balcony. Go bike riding or go for a walk every day to smell the flowers, look up at the sky, and contemplate the vastness and awe of creation that you are a part of. Create a daily practice of gratitude and watch the magic unfold in your life.

Enjoy your life more, and more money will come. That's the crazy paradox of it all. You think you have to force and push to make it all work. Instead, while you're having fun, keep one eye open for synchronicity showing up to guide you to your next step.

Be a Continual Student of Success

"Like a bee that seeks nectar from all kinds of flowers, seek teachings everywhere. Like a deer that chooses a quiet field to graze, seek seclusion that you may digest all that you have learned. Like a mad one beyond all limits, live like a lion, completely free of all fear."

That is my all-time favorite quote. I once heard it on a yoga CD. I have my favorite quote beautifully decorated on a nice piece of paper hanging on my wall where I can see it every day.

Like any great success story in life, it all started for me with a desire to learn, so become a continual student of success. Get a mentor – someone you trust, someone whose information is valuable to you, and someone who can help you take those next steps to grow your business and help you achieve the freedom, abundance, and joy you deserve.

I have many mentors. I love learning! I am addicted to learning. I have books, audio programs, and binders full of fabulous knowledge at my fingertips when I need them. As they say, knowledge is power.

It's so important to have a mentor or to follow someone who can guide you. You need to look to someone who has been in the trenches and has come out alive and prosperous on the other side. You can't do it alone, plain and simple. If life and success were meant to be lived and enjoyed alone there wouldn't be six billion people on this earth.

Cultivate and Cherish a Community of Like-Minded People

Ideas are easy; what's challenging are implementing those ideas and having the discipline to continue implementing and working on your projects once the initial thrill and the idea of growing your business has worn out.

"...What most of us don't realize is that our fear of discipline causes us to sell our souls and forfeit our dreams."

– Debbie Ford

I also suggest you get a mastermind group of people together (or even one other person) to connect with on a regular basis with the objectives of bouncing ideas off of one another, and supporting and encouraging one another on the road to success.

It's so nice to know someone believes in you. Sometimes just having that one person to hold you accountable will give you the kick in the pants to take continual action.

A mastermind group is formed when two or more people of like-mind get together to support each other's vision of success. It is so powerful and, I think, a real necessity for anyone engaged in any kind of business.

Some of the relationships I cherish dearly were formed through mastermind groups. I believe that magic happens when you commit to a group of people your intentions for success.

I hope my story and the information contained in this book have inspired you to take action in the direction of your dreams toward more prosperity, freedom, and fulfillment.

All the success in the world is out there for you. You just have to invite it in.

To Your Love, Expansion and Freedom,

Words of Appreciation and Resources

"My Testimonial Is a Really Big Thank You!"

Vanessa is a voice of reason in my often chaotic life and head. When I get the chance to speak with Vanessa, no matter what the subject or the problem at hand, she helps me see clearly and puts into words what I'd been trying to formulate for God knows how long.

The Law of Attraction is something everyone in the world should know about, and Vanessa is the one who should tell them about it. Her words are strong and full of conviction, and even if you don't want to listen, she'll make you simply by promoting what she believes in the most; the power to be who you want to be and do what you want to do, no matter who you are or where you are in life.

My life has changed so dramatically since I met Vanessa, I'm not even sure how to put it into words. All I can say is that it's been nothing but good things! Thank you, thank you, thank you!

Miranda Lightstone
Editor/Writer
Montreal, Quebec

"You Helped Us Reach Our Goals!"

The very first thing that struck me about Vanessa was her unique presence: She has this aura and wonderful personality about her. She easily communicates her belief in the product she sells, and I believe that's what really sells.

Standing back and watching her shows, I noticed that she always took the time to focus 100% on her clients and made them feel like they were the only ones that mattered to her in the world.

She puts her heart and enthusiasm into her work and delivers her sales presentation with this calm confidence and presence that people can't get enough of! Even her voice is very soothing, and people are naturally curious when they hear her announcements and come (literally) running to fill their curiosity!

Thank you for bringing your fabulous presence to the store and for helping us reach our sales goals!

Stan Streholm
Retail Store Manager
Moncton, New Brunswick

"You Became a Positive Inspiration to Us All!"

From the very first moment I met Vanessa Simpkins at an audition, I knew that she was unique. She definitely stood out from the other candidates. She was totally riveting and dynamic, and asked questions that most candidates hadn't considered or were too shy to ask.

I knew immediately: That girl will be great! And great she was!

The agents who do well in this company must have a positive attitude, even if they are having a bad day. Vanessa went beyond positive and became an inspiration to all of us!

She used the Law of Attraction not only for sales and to draw to her booth positive, excited customers who were willing to buy. We all marvel at her phenomenal sales skills.

I am honoured to be a part of her book, and I know without a doubt that this book, along with everything I have witnessed Vanessa accomplish, will be remarkable!

Lori Couture
Manager
Eastern Canada

"Your Motivation Is Very Contagious!"

Your motivation is very contagious. You are very wise for such a young woman. Working with you has allowed me to dig deeper into what I want and what I don't want – not what I should or should not want, and always considering everybody else first before myself. You could spend hours with a psychologist and never feel that you're making progress. In a very short period, you managed to clarify some very important issues for me. Thank you!

Sandra MacDougall
Real Estate Agent
Montreal Quebec

"A Source of Inspiration to Me"

Vanessa has always been a source of inspiration to me, her clear head and concise manner of speaking are really motivating! A year ago I was just treading water and had almost no idea how I would get from where I was to starting my service Web business, but with Vanessa's help, today I am completely self employed and loving every minute of it. Vanessa gave me the kick in the pants I needed, and gave me to tools to find clarity and define my goals and most importantly, go after them. I never liked the idea of going after "money" or "fame" but she taught me that when you work hard and genuinely care about helping people, the money comes naturally and guilt free. Thank you Vanessa for all your attention and pant kicking!

Georgiana Laudi
www.GiaWorks.com

"Vanessa Completely Astounded me From the Get-Go"

I had a ton of passion and thought I could be good at sales and marketing, but I couldn't focus on what I needed to be doing. I've worked closely with Vanessa and every call we have together makes me money because of the laser clarity and direction she consistently offers me! It's totally incredible! Connecting with Vanessa was the most brilliant thing I ever did for my sanity and my business!

Marci Lebowitz
www.MarciLebowitz.com
Chicago, USA

"I am Not Frantically Run by my Emotions Anymore!"

Before working with Vanessa, I felt stuck, and trapped in this endless busyness cycle all the time. I sacrificed having fun, I skipped meals and let my health slip, I never had time for myself or my loved ones. I was tired all the time and had no energy and constantly worried about where the next sale would come from in my company.

Coaching with Vanessa has been A RIDE!! I now get to spend more time with my friends, my family and actually get better results at work! I closed a a HUGE contract with a fabulous client for $30,000, and it happened exactly the way I visualized it! I now I know that my heart vibrates and creates my reality.

I've learnt that changes come from the inside and the world conspires to give you what you want! I feel happy again! My health is on track, everyone at work can see the difference in me, and I am celebrating all the big and small things that happen everyday! I am not frantically run by my emotions anymore - I am creating, fully aware and living now! I feel alive and excitement everyday at what will show up next! Thank you for this AMAZING ride!!!

Silvia Zoch
Sales Director

"I had one session with Vanessa and it changed my life!"

Vanessa helped me overcome fear that has kept me from driving a vehicle for over 5 yrs. I got into a pretty bad accident a while back and was too frightened to get back behind the wheel of a car. After one VERY powerful session with Vanessa I am thrilled because I am driving again! I got my license and bought a car and am now FREE! I am able to drive to my clients and that opens up a whole new world of possibility and more income for me! Thank you Vanessa!

Bella Cadotte
Photographer
www.BellaStardust.com

Get Your Companion Audios, Video, PDF Guide & Meditation
Over $597.00 Value – Yours <u>FREE</u>

<u>Bonus #1</u> - FREE Audio - **"Inside Sales Tips: 5 Sizzling Strategies to Help You Sell More Authentically and Effectively"** - $97
Featuring America's Sales Attraction Coach, Vanessa Simpkins
Listen to this companion audio and discover:

1) 1) The single most important reason why most people never excel in sales. (Never fall prey to it again!)
2) 2) Mindset Mastery. How to stop sabotaging yourself and "getting in your own way" when it comes to selling.
3) 3) Five Simple strategies that will allow you to increase your sales while having more fun than you've ever imagined possible.
4) 4) Insider secrets to selling more authentically and effectively that will turn your sales process from "blah" to "rock your socks off" amazing.
5) 5) Three Proven Methods to "close more sales more easily" for selling and marketing-phobes and those who are stuck at YUK when thinking of selling.

<u>Bonus #2</u> – **Vanessa's Personal Guided Meditation & Visualization** - $37
Listen to this meditation and discover:

1) How to release emotional blocks from the energetic body quickly and easily so you can amp up your vibration with a positive frequency for success.
2) Learn exactly which organ in your body manages specific emotions and how to permanently reprogram your energy system with supportive emotions.
3) Connect with the highest vision of your future self and allow you higher power to help you discover, uncover and transform yourself into your true vision of success with guided visualization.

Bonus #3 - **Video + PDF Guide- $ 97 Value Yours FREE**
Watch this video and discover:

1) Vanessa's Secret Weapon for Manifesting with Success. Learn exactly how she went from Bankrupt to making $900 a day, wrote her first book and launched a successful coaching career in under 2 years all by using this simple writing exercise.
2) How to stop struggling, pushing and forcing life to bend your way. Find out how you can apply this one simple process that takes less than 15 minutes a day to help you attract your perfect clients, business partners or investors and help you close more sales more easily and make more money quickly by aligning you with what you want so it flows smoothly into your experience.
3) A step-by-step PDF guide to help you start writing your very own blueprint for success, pronto!

Bonus # 4 – **Coupon for $200 off of your Big Breakthrough Session with Vanessa**
In your Big Breakthrough Session with Vanessa you will:

1) Discover how to release your energetic blocks once and for all and allow more wealth into your life.
2) Master the inner mindset for gaining more confidence and doubling, tripling or even quadrupling your sales.
3) Learn how to naturally align yourself with your ideal clients so you attract your perfect clients, have more fun and get paid for enjoying yourself and doing what you do best
4) Help you develop your own unique and authentic selling style that looks and feels right for you so you enjoy the process, close more sales more easily and make more money.
5) Conquer the outer strategies and sales techniques that will help you sky-rocket your sales conversion and grow your business so you can make more money and enjoy a fabulous lifestyle with the freedom to choose how you spend your time.

Get all 6 FREE Bonuses today at
www.TakeYourPowerBackNow.com/bonus

<u>Bonus #5</u> - **Expert Interview with Brad Yates – Emotional Freedom Technique (EFT) Practitioner, Author and Professional Speaker - $97**

Listen to this audio and discover:

1) How to tap into your passion and purpose using EFT (Emotional Freedom Technique) one of the most popular and effective energy psychology tool s out there!
2) Eliminate your anxiety and limiting beliefs about making money in these challenging economic times so you can start to prosper and enjoy more money and freedom.
3) Learn a simple technique for releasing emotional resistance you can do on your own and in as little time as a few minutes.

<u>Bonus #6</u> - **Expert Interview with Dr. Joe Vitale star of "The Secret" and Spiritual Marketing Guru. Get the Transcription and Accelerated PDF Work Guide to help you Achieve Success Today! $97**

Listen to this audio and discover:

1) The real reason most people never find their passion or purpose in life, and how to overcome it quickly.
2) How a simple breakthrough clearing process will help you catapult your success in your sales career and help you grow your business like never before.
3) How to release self-sabotage once and for all in as little as seconds, even if you haven't a clue that you are doing it and without spending years in therapy.

Get all 6 FREE Bonuses today at
www.TakeYourPowerBackNow.com/bonus

About the Author
Vanessa Simpkins

"Authenticity is the new currency in business today."

- Vanessa

Vanessa Simpkins is a sky rocket your confidence & cash flow mentor, speaker and author of "From Bankrupt to $900 a Day Selling Mops". Creator of the "Transformational Breakthrough Summit" Vanessa helps entrepreneurs breakthrough their inner blocks, skyrocket their confidence and put proven systems in place to attract more clients and make more money. She's been featured in "Motivated Magazine", "Today's Business Women Magazine", worked alongside personal development experts like Joe Vitale from the hit Movie "The Secret" & Marci Shimoff from "Happy for No Reason" and has also spoken at the TED EX "Let's Spread Success" event in Montreal. Vanessa loves teaching authentic success principals that empower and inspire **Personal & Professional FREEDOM ** to help entrepreneurs & sales professionals create a life and business by design instead of by default. To find out more about her workshops in Costa Rica, USA and Canada and to get your FREE audio "How to Sky Rocket Your Confidence & Cash Flow: 5 of the Biggest Money, Mindset and Power Leaks Entrepreneurs Make and How to Avoid Them" visit her websitewww.TakeYourPowerBackNow.com.

Vanessa has changed my life in ways I can't even begin to describe! Before I met her I was totally dissatisfied with my life, in debt and hopping from job to job. Following her lead and this contagious happiness she exudes has literally turned my life right around to the point where I don't even recognize myself. I've quadrupled my income, lived my dream and traveled to Hawaii. Most of all, I know now (really know!) how to manifest whatever I want. Vanessa, I just want to say thanks from the bottom of my heart!

Melanie Layer
Regional Sales Trainer
St. Jerome Quebec, Canada